POLLY'S PARLOUR

Based on true events

Twisted with Love & Darkness.

ISBN-9798333628558

Cover design by Lee West & Emma Jade Reed photography.
Library of Congress Control Number: 2018675309
Printed in the United States of America

POLLY'S PARLOUR

Lee West

Brighton, England 1999.

CHAPTER ONE

Gary

During this present day, in the sweltering summer sun of 1999, in a cemetery on the edge of Brighton, England, a burial is taking place, with everyone tense & silent. The sun is pouring its boiling waves onto the sweaty attendees, some of whom are head to toe in black for a fashion statement, rather than it being heart felt mourning attire. Thus, attracting the heat, with some of them wishing this body burying would hurry up. Whilst a coffin is lowered into the ground and people crying, Pauline lifts her black veil, wipes her face and in the corner of her eye sees a car with blacked out windows driving past, slowly. Suspicious of it, she stares, the window comes down, Pauline's face is stunned when she sees who it is, smiles gently, pulls her veil back down over her face and bows her head.

Two weeks previously, Pauline, a well-known Madame, 40, with shoulder-length blonde hair, tanned, tall, with a pretty face, is getting out of her Range Rover. Dressed in denim skirt, bright red top, high heels, huge hoop earrings & denim jacket, she has arrived home from a night out. Holding a lit cigarette in one hand, bags in the other, she walks towards steps outside of a four story georgian building.

Neighbour upstairs watering window sill plants is looking over and waiting for Pauline to get closer.

Nicki who is late 40's, covered in tattoos, cold green eyes, short, very thin with a shaved head, proudly has a rainbow flag hanging in her window, raises her voice at Pauline.

"Dog's dinner springs to mind."

"Fuck off Nicki and get back in your cage."

"With all the howling going on in your place last night anyone would think I live above an animal rescue centre."

"At least my girls are getting it. Better to live a lubricated life than a dried up shrivelled one."

"Shrivelled like your old chesterfield face."

"Not as ancient as you though, am I Nicki?"

Nicki feeling smug. "You wouldn't know, I never actually told you my real age."

"You didn't need to - your baggy neck gives it away."

"You vile piece of..."

"Now now, Nicki. Too much gob will give me enough room to put my fist inside it."

"After everything I did for you."

"Did for me?" Pauline shouts.

"I worked my ass off and you got rid of me, with no notice."

As Nicki pulls a sad, but sarcastic face, Pauline's blood starts to boil and yells very loudly;

"Notice? I'll give you some extended annual leave though - see it as a 30 year holiday, with no return. I let you go because all the men said you were hideous in bed. Yes, that's right neighbourhood; Nicki was fired because of her fanny - or lack of it."

"I put loads of my time and energy into that place."

"I would need to hook you up to the national grid to get any energy out of you."

"That's crap and you know it."

"You're just a skeleton that breathes, and even that's annoying."

Nicki is bright red and shuts window, banging her head in the process. Pauline walks down some steps towards her apartment, laughing.

Polly's Parlour is a three-bed apartment, with one small office room, in the basement, with concrete steps winding down to her own front door, with a pink neon light displaying; "Polly's Parlour. Professional massage and international learning centre."

Inside is crushed red velvet curtains, wooden floors, big lamps, dim lights, classy, has a calming vibe and *always* clean. Pauline walks in and is immediately irritated at the smell.

The girls working for her throughout the night are Layla, 30, hook nose, sketchy, loud, long black tied back hair, parties too much. Alongside is Sheila, 19, soft, timid, adorable nature, bohemian, peroxide blonde with roots, and Lisa, receptionist, 25, blonde, bubbly, smiles a lot, loves money. Pauline stamps her tone with absolute authority.

"Oooiiii, wake up. Smells like a rough whorehouse in here."

Pauline pulls open the curtains. Layla and Sheila are asleep on floor, surrounded by chocolate wrappers, empty alcohol bottles, a full ashtray and sex toys. Sheila is curled up sucking her thumb, Layla in a Wonder Woman outfit. Gabrielle's album, *Rise*, is playing quietly in the background. "Layla, wake up. Sheila, get yourself up and washed, now."

"What? What time is it?" Layla snaps.

"Suck-a-cock-time is what it is, now move it. First client will be here in less than an hour. Where the hell is Lisa?"

Sheila starts to open her eyes and yawns as she speaks.

"Morning Polly. Sorry we had a drink after we finished. Lisa is asleep in one of the bedrooms."

"Right, you two, get up, get freshened up and get your uniforms on."

"What uniforms?" Asks Sheila.

"Cheerleaders, both of you. That American is back to see you both."

Layla fails to hold in her real feelings, as per normal.
"Again? That's the third time this week. For fuck's sake."

With no hesitation Pauline quips.

"If you don't want to work here then piss off, I can find plenty more tarts in this town. I'm sick of you girls not being ready. Get your pompoms out, he wants you to chant his mother's name today, don't ask."

Pauline leaves room without a word.

"Oh my God, Layla, his mum's name?"

"It better not be a long one, that's way too much chanting."

"Stop. Don't make me laugh again. He was furious last time."

"I can't help it, those knickers he wears, I mean, what the..."

"Maybe they were his mum's."

Covering her mouth & running towards the bathroom.

"I'm gonna be sick."

Pauline strides towards and enters one of the bedrooms by kicking the door open.
"Aww morning honey. WAKE UUUUP."

Whilst Lisa covers her ears - "Holy crap Polly. I'm sorry I just..."

"Clean this place up and get on the front desk. I've got a new girl coming to look round later, so make it look less...whore-ish"

"Of course, yeah, I'm so sorry, I never over sleep. That bloody wine went to my head. The girls and I just wanted to let loose when we finished."

"I gathered. That twat upstairs has already complained about the noise."

"Sorry. It was a one off as we had a big tip, so wanted to

celebrate."

"I'm assuming you've put back my share?"

"Um, yeah, yeah of course. It's in the lounge with the girls, I think."

"Who gave the tip?"

"Pissy Pete."

"Why was he so generous? He's usually tighter than his nappy."

"Said he won it or something."

"How much?"

"Never said."

"I mean how much was the tip?"

"Ah, 300."

"Wow, great. Get some coffee in you and get those pillow creases out of your face. Don't want my punters put off, we've got a busy day." Pauline leaves room and walks back towards the lounge, leaving Lisa confused as she looks in the mirror at perfectly fine skin.

"Oh." Lisa exhales.

As Pauline walks towards the lounge she looks through the crack of another bedroom door and eavesdrops, as she watches Layla and Sheila, just as Layla is snorting a line of something.

"Layla you should give that up, it's not good for you and she'll kill you if she finds out."

"She won't. She met me when I was wired, so she's never known me any different."

"I worry about you."

"Listen kid, I've been around the block a lot longer than you, you're young, you won't understand. I can't do it without it, it numbs the..."

"Numbs the?"

"Nothing Sheila, just, pass the pompoms, let's practice our synchronicity."

Both do a synchronised high leg kick and laugh. Pauline walks back to reception with a slight smile.

Half an hour later Polly's Parlour is buzzing with girls getting ready, music playing, phone ringing and Pauline making sure all the fine details are to her standard, as she rubs her fingers along the side cabinets checking for dust.

The main hub being the reception, which has a modern glass and wooden curved high desk, chandelier above, neat, tidy, tip jar and bowl of condoms on the top. Lisa is scoffing a huge bar of chocolate, and has a mouth full, whilst making annoying noises. Pauline looks on in dismay.

"What on earth are you doing?"

"Eating my feelings. Want some?"

"Far too early for chocolate. What feelings?"

"Just crap from my past, you know how it is, especially when hungover. Makes everything feel sad."

"Money outweighs trauma any day, Lisa. You keep putting the hours in and you'll have a nice life. The past will always be there, but let it breathe in the present and you'll get nowhere, it will make you unwell. Push it away, enjoy being independent, you know I'm always here for you." Lisa half smiles as she is still eating. Pauline takes a call on the Parlour phone as Lisa starts to fold up towels in the hallway.

"Hello Polly's Parlour. Yes that's correct, 48 Welbeck Street. We have two girls on today and possibly three this evening. Blonde? Yes, I'm sure that will be ok, one second."

Pauline puts her hand over the phone and whispers to Lisa.

"Want some extra bucks?"

"Depends."

"Just a few sniffs of your knickers, lay back, he will sort himself out."

"I don't wear any though." Lisa announces proudly.

"Ugh, really? Not even when sitting on my new chair?"

"No. I love the breeze up there."

"Disgusting. I've got a pair that you can wear, don't worry they're clean."

"Yeah, ok, just this once though."

Pauline rolls her eyes. "Not heard you say that before."

"I've never done any..."

Pauline cuts her up mid flow and with a smirk, talks back into phone. "Yes Sir, we have a luscious lady here for you who will let you inhale the scent of her lovely labia. Yes she's blonde, buxom and, pardon? Um, hang on one sec let me ask."

"Psstt, Lisa, will you sit on his face?"

"Ummm. I'm not sure I...."

Again Pauline abruptly cuts her up. "Yes she will, great see you at 12 sharp, sweet heart."

Lisa looks dumbfounded but gets the confidence to speak up.

"Polly, I don't want to be a working girl, I like being the receptionist."

"You said that last time, and the time before. You need money for some underwear so." Pauline takes her knickers off and throws them at Lisa. Lisa catches them with much trepidation. Pauline brazenly carries on. "Here, put these on, don't wash, he wants it all sweaty down there."

"But you said they were clean."

"They are, sort of. Don't back chat, get on with it."

The door buzzer sound makes Pauline jump. Pauline speaks on the intercom. "Yes, how can I help?"

Pissy Pete is at the door, shirt and tie, looking sweaty, hungover and grey skinned.

"Hi it's Pete, is that Polly?"

"Sure is, what's up?"

"Can I speak to you indoors please?"

"My time isn't free babe, you know that."

"Ok, can I book half an hour."

"Nope, only charge by the hour."

"Oh, ummm, let me thi..."

Pauline being too impatient, buzzes him in anyway, as he's thinking and stuttering. Pete is in his 30's, slightly awkward, glasses, charming smile, but looks scared. "Hey, Polly, sorry, I just, can we go somewhere private?"

"Yep, come into my office." Pauline holds her hand out for the cash, he pays her and she puts it in her bra as they both walk into office and shut the door.

Office is a small room at the back of the apartment, desk with stack of files on top, dark, has a hidden cash stash safe, but used mostly for storing sex toys & outfits. Pauline perches seductively on the desk and leans in, with cleavage so obviously pushed out for maximum effect.

"Take a seat. How are you? Not seen you for a few weeks." Pauline says sexually, close to his ear.

"I was here last night, don't you remember?"

"I wasn't here last night, I was at an all night orgy. I'm shattered."

"Wow, an orgy. You have sex with lots of men then?"

"No, I run it and keep it all in order. I'm more of a spectator. I save myself for special moments to be honest, you know me well enough to know that."

"Like?"

Pauline starts to heat things up and slides the denim jacket off of her shoulders to reveal a beautiful, intricate, spiritual, tattoo - all over her shoulder, running down to her left breast, licking her lips at the same time.

"When the price is right I'll happily let someone......enter Polly's tunnel, if you, get my drift."

Pete starts to unbutton his top button and sweats even more. "Is it hot in here? I'm, ummm, can I just, need to back track, last

9

night, I was here and lost loads of money."

"Lost? This isn't the bloody Brighton casino."

"I don't remember much and I don't do drugs, so I think my drink must have been spiked."

"Are you suggesting in my Parlour there is foul play?"

"Polly, I don't want to upset you, I love coming here. I've just never blacked out before and I had plenty in my wallet as I won a bet at the races. Woke up with only 150 in my wallet."

"How much you win?"

"A grand."

Pauline visibly feels let down as she was expecting him to have won more. "Ah, I thought you were going to say thousands."

"It feels like thousands, I'm not rich. I only booked one hour so I would have plenty left, but it's all hazy."

"I'm sure it'll turn up or you'll get your memory back. I don't allow drugs here and my girls aren't thieves. They may be a bit dodgy at times, but druggies and thieves they are not."

"Look, I don't want to get anyone into any trouble, can you just ask them what happened please?"

Pauline seems irritated at having to deal with this, so shouts out, "Girls, in here now please." Lisa walks in holding Pauline's knickers, Layla and Sheila still half dressing into pink & white cheerleader jackets. Layla has walked in with a bit an attitude, sniffs twice and seems a bit hyper.

"What now? Oh, hello, nice to see you again so soon."

"Pete here seems to be a bit short on cash after a visit here last night. Anyone know anything about this?"

Sheila, in her soft voice, speaks up first.

"Pete, you handed us some money after you drank bubbly and you gave it to us as big thank-you tip."

"What bubbly?"

"You won 4 bottles at the races and brought them here to drink with us. You had already had one bottle at the races, you said. It was that Cava stuff and you drank most of it, danced and passed out, so I put you in a taxi. You gave us a big tip because you said you'd never made your nappy so wet after we finished in the bedroom."

"Did I?" looking confused at her reply.

Layla, very abruptly takes over. "I can get it out of the bloody bin if you don't believe us, take a look for yourself."

Bright red in the cheeks and looking at all the girls, Pete stutters his words. "No, no, it's fine. It's just, I've never not remembered what's happened when I drink."

"Ever had Cava before?" Layla quips.

"Well, no, I..."

"There you go, problem solved - Cava doesn't agree with you. Now, can we get on with our work please?"

Pauline glares at Layla. "Yes, off you go girls."

As all three exit, Layla skips her way out looking like she's coming up on drugs and Pauline bites her tongue and turns her attention to Pete. "Listen, Pete, you're one of my most valued customers."

Pete's mood changes. "I'm not happy, something is off. If word got around about this."

Pauline goes from 0-100 in a split second.

"Don't go there with me pal. One call and you'll have no bowels left to empty here. So I suggest you keep your paranoid blackouts away from my door, my livelihood."

Pete realises he's over-stepped the mark, and tries to suck up to Pauline. "Ok sorry, really, sorry. I'll stick to beer. I'm just hungover. Sorry.

"You can go now."

"What? I've got 45 minutes left. What can I have?"

"The girls are busy, so I can only offer hand relief for now."

"I would rather have a spanking to be honest." Again Pete tries to be brave and squares up to Paulines's face and grabs her arm. "You remember the good old days eh Polly? You loved a bit of roughness didn't you?"

"Take that fucking hand off of my arm, NOW. Listen to me, pissy pants, here, have this." Pauline hands him a small card.

"What the hell is this?"

"It's a voucher for a free half an hour, now get out of here. If you can't handle your drink then don't come here drunk. End of."

"Fine. I will return for a mother and baby session another day."

"Buy some sudocrem. I've heard you've got a nasty rash down there."

"What the fuck, Polly." Pete gives her a filthy look and slams the door on his way out.

Pauline goes to one of the bedrooms to check on Layla and Sheila. "Right, come on you two dolls, let me have a look at you." Pauline tightens a hair bunch of Layla's and straightens Sheila's collar.
"My, my, what lovely innocent girls you are, aren't you?"
Just as Layla beams with a smile, Pauline grabs Layla's chin with force.
"What's that white shit on your nose?"

"Washing powder. I was just smelling that new tropical one you bought."

"Is that right? I'm on to you young lady. What do you think?"

"I think it'll definitely get all the stains out of the sheets, it's really lovely."

"I meant what do you think of Pete's money situation."

"Oh, well I really have no idea why he can't..."

"Shhhhhh. Settle yourself, you talk too much. You know if I find out it's coke on your conk of a nose you'll be out of here? You will never work here again, understand?"

Sheila's timid tone interrupts Pauline. "I was with her when..."

"Be quiet and brush your teeth, your breath stinks."

"Sorry."

"So what's the drill girls?"

Sheila proudly describes her knowledge of this routine.

"So, when he comes in we start marching on the spot in silence."

"Then?"

Excitedly Sheila continues.

"Then we march over to him when he sits on the bed and stare into his eyes and smile, whilst still marching, as he starts to undress himself. Then we stand back and when he's fully naked, apart from his weird knickers, we do star jumps and yell in an American accent;

"Give me an..." And spell out whatever name he gives us."

"Well done darling, nice to see you're on the ball. As before he will hand you the name on a piece of paper as he comes in. He wants other things today, not just a hand job with the pompoms ok."

"Like what?" Layla bites.

"God knows, just be prepared. He will be here shortly. Now, you be good American girls for Momma Polly won't ya?" Says Pauline in a Southern American accent. All three smile and Pauline looks at them with pride, kisses them both on the forehead and exits the bedroom.

Pauline picks up bag of rubbish and takes it outside to her bins and notices a small removal van with a rival Madame, Belinda, taking in bags of clothes to an apartment, five doors down.

Belinda, an old enemy, with lots of history, is a tall transvestite, late 50's, wears a brown wig that looks like its made out of horse hair, has thick orange foundation and tight jeans. Belinda, with big hands, looks like a builder in a floral blouse which is too tight.

Pauline sarcastically grins as she walks towards Belinda and looks her up and down with utter disgust.

"Well, well, well. If it isn't the old trollop Belinda."

"Might have known you'd come out to have a nose."

"I'm not here to view your bags of charity shop clothes. I'm here to tell you this is my street, my business, so best you not get any ideas in that meat head of yours. Crossing me once was more than you should take on. Cross me again and you'll need a carer the rest of your life."

"Here we go again. Do you ever give that gob a rest. This was the only place up for rent since you got my last place shut down."

"Tearing my girls' cards down out of the phone boxes and replacing them with those cheap hookers who work for you, was a huge mistake."

Pauline almost spitting out of her mouth with anger and gets up close to Belinda.

Belinda flinches and takes step back and takes a puff on her cigarette, blowing it in Pauline's face.

"Someone grassed on my last two businesses and got them closed down. You're the only one who would do that to me."

"Underage girls and running drugs would have got you closed, not having a reputable house. I don't say shit to the police, never have, never will. I don't want you in business around here, you give this profession a bad name."

"There's enough room for two of us. Besides, I have a niche market, you don't."

Pauline tilts her head back laughing.

"Niche? Keep your old folks and their £30 'quickies'. Step on my toes one more time and I'll burn your fucking brothel down, along with all your fake designer gear, and you'll not have anywhere to work from. I'll have someone monitoring the call boxes and making sure you aren't stood out here hustling and stealing my punters."

Belinda adjusts her bra strap and flicks her cigarette butt past Pauline, nearly hitting her.

"Shut up, you don't run this neighbourhood. I've as much right to be here."

"This is your last warning. Don't fuck with me again, ever."

Belinda tries to stand up to her, but she isn't a match and she knows it, so scuttles off quickly as she calls back. "I'm really trembling Pauline, grow up."

Pauline raises her voice. "Trust me, Bell-end, I will come for you."

Belinda slams her door as Pauline's rage shows in her face as she walks back into Polly's Parlour.

Pauline stands at the front of reception and starts to chat to Lisa, who's behind the desk perched on a black and silver high stool, which spins. Lisa spins herself around fast, twice, with a huge smile and high-pitched giggle, which breaks Pauline's mood and makes her smile.

Pauline presses buzzer and lets in a punter. Jay, an American buff man, hair slicked to one side, handsome, in an all American college type jacket, walks towards Pauline with a grin from ear to ear. In a clear attempt to try and sound American, he goes over the top and sounds more Irish;

"Well, howdy Polly. What a beautiful and glorious day it is."

"Sure is honey, lovely to see you again. Settle with Lisa and go on through to the bedroom. The cheerleaders are waiting on the side lines." Jay pays Lisa and walks off to the bedroom.

Pauline turns to Lisa.

"Never guess who's pitched up on this street, that baggy Belinda. Grates on me that one."

"So it is true?"

"What's true?"

"I heard she was going to set up a dungeon type of brothel around here and cater for the old kinky men."

"Great, that's all I need is the leather parade drawing attention on this street. I can just picture it; fucking ass everywhere, hanging out of leather chaps. I've warned her - a final warning in fact. Anyway, enough of that, there are bigger things to worry about right now."

"Such as?"

"Lisa, I've got something to tell you. Please don't repeat this."

"You know me, I never open my mouth."

"Unless it's for money right? Listen, I'm going to hire a security guard for a while, just for the evenings."

"What? Why? What's happened?"

"That guy I've been seeing, he's only bloody gangster Gary."

"Tania's ex? Not seen her for ages come to think of it."

"Me neither, I've heard she's been abroad but she's back apparently. I need to call her, definitely after this morning's antics. I didn't put two and two together but it clicked when we were in bed."

"What happened?" Lisa worriedly whispers.

"After the all night orgy I called in to see him on my way here for an hour. We were having a lovely passionate time in bed and all of a sudden he left my front porch and started putting his hands by my... you know." Pauline points to her behind.

"Oh God. Then what?"

"He exploded, like I've never seen, then I remembered, in that moment, what Tania used to say; Gary would shoot like a fountain when he did that to her. She told me other stuff ages ago but I can't recall all of it. This morning was the first time since I met him a month ago. He's trouble and I mean BIG trouble. I just felt so uncomfortable."

"Who wouldn't feel uncomfortable with a man at their back door."

"No, I mean, just uncomfortable in his presence. I remember Tania saying once he's seeing someone he claims them as his, like a trophy, and is constantly paranoid about honesty. He becomes obsessive when he feels insecure and just a few things he's said this week have made me feel like he's on to me."

16

"About what?"

"About my business. I've fed him a story of being a landlady, not a bloody Madame running my own adult Parlour. He's asked so many times to stay over at my place, but I fob him off all the time and this morning he was persistent about spending time with me but I've told him I have family staying."

"You really like him though, don't you?"

"That's the problem Lisa. I've lied so many times to him this past month and if he finds out he will hate that he's been seeing a Madame. I'm worried, but I like him a lot, which baffles me. You know me, I don't ever meet anyone I go silly over, but him, different kettle of fish. I just wanted to find a man who wants me for me and sees beyond the Parlour. There was a car just like his tailing a few cars behind this morning after I left his. I thought it was him, or maybe I'm just over tired and paranoid."

"You're probably just tired. You've been up all night guarding the fetish fort. Can't you walk away and just see it as a nice short fling? Or tell him the truth?"

Pauline looks deep in thought and almost worried, and does not answer her.

"Polly, are you alright? Feels like you want to say something."

"I wish it was that easy. You see he doesn't know about....." In the background are chants from the girls, which over powers Pauline's voice, so Lisa and Pauline can't help but listen.

In a very convincing cheerleading energetic American shout, Sheila and Layla yell from the bedroom;

"Let's go team. Give me an M, give me an A, give me an R, give me a G, give me an A, give me an R, give me an E, give me a T. That's right, it's your Momma Margaret, your Momma Margaret - Yay, hip hip, hooray." A blow of their whistles is followed by Jay's almighty orgasmic groans, as if he was coming for England. Pauline nods her head at Lisa.

"Jesus Christ, I'll tell you more later, DON'T mention this to anyone, let me figure it out."

"You have my word. I swear on my Nan's...oh no she died already, umm, swear on my mum's life."

Pauline's brick mobile phone rings. "Speak of the devil." Pauline goes through to the kitchen whilst answering the phone.

The girls let Jay out and chat to Lisa at reception, Layla wiping something off of her chin, asks Lisa a question; "Who's she on the phone with?"

"Probably Sandra ringing in sick, again."

"She better not be, I need tonight off to go to that party on the seafront. Sheila go and listen in, you're less conspicuous than me."

Pauline is on the phone in kitchen, has her back to the doorway, so Sheila gets close and listens in.

"I'm just at work collecting rent from my tenants and then I have a few errands to run. Of course I'm at work, where else would I be, silly. Are you alright? Sound a bit pissed off?"

Pauline starts to feel anxious and it shows on her face for Sheila to see. Pauline notices her in the corner of her eye, but does not let her know she has seen her, so becomes flippant on the phone. "I've got to go, yes 8pm is perfect, see you there, babe."

"Night out?"

"Yep, just a few drinks in that new bar in Kemptown, nothing fancy. How was Jay?"

"Quick, very quick. I had to pretend to breast feed him. Wonder why so fascinated by his mum?"

"That's none of our business, we aren't counsellors."

"Just amazes me really."

"We've got a new girl coming in soon, mate of Sandra's."

"Not that Leigh is it?"

"You know her?"

"Sort of. She worked the lane up in Leeds, I was there for a few weeks before moving down here."

"What were you doing up there?"

"I was working the lane and worked for a guy I liked but thing's got strange so I jumped the train down south. Leigh was a tough lass up there, everyone was scared of her."

"I see. You've never told me much about your past. Well, you're safer in here than out there."

"Thank you, Polly."

"Just greet her and make her feel welcome. Actually, girls, listen. Right, new girl coming to look round shortly and if she likes it she will start tonight with Sandra. Anyone like any over time? I'm off out tonight."

"Another orgy?" Layla quips and sniffs, thinking she's funny.

Pauline glares at Layla, as if to look straight through her. "No, thank you, it's date night, but, I may call it off with Gary."

Layla looking puzzled. "How come? Thought you really liked him? Aren't we going to meet him then? Sheila has met him."

"No. That was a one off. I like to keep my private life separate and away from here. I like him, but it's....fractured." Looks at Lisa with affection. "Lisa, you ok to come back in tonight and do reception please?"

"Yeah sure. Ching, Ching Miss ping-a-ling."

Pauline's laughter takes hold, with a small snort at the end. "I swear you are on something, you come out with some random shit don't you. I've got to go out and sort a few things, so eyes and ears to the ground for me as always please Lisa."

Layla smirks at her in a sarcastic way. "I will stay on until 8ish, got a party to go to. Got a date too."

Pauline intrigued. "Whoohh, Miss Frosty Knickers may finally find love."

"As if."

"Now you girls be ready and on time for each punter today. I'll be back in a couple of hours."

As Pauline leaves the flat, the knicker sniffer arrives for Lisa. Josh, 35, is handsome, tattoos, a bit nervous, dapper in a fitted dark blue three-piece suit, hands Lisa the money.

"Hello, thank you. Come on through." Lisa nervously welcomes him.

Both enter the bedroom and out of nowhere Lisa just pulls her skirt down straight away, leaving Josh stunned.
"Oh, crikey. I have a pair with me I would like you to wear, if that's alright?"

Lisa is blushing beyond red and tinkering on purple, with veins in side of head pulsating through embarrassment and fear.
"Um, sure. I thought you might like these."

"Not really, no. Not at all in fact."

"Wow, brutal. Well, for the record - they aren't mine anyway."

"Please, don't put me off more than I already am." Josh gives a massive cheeky grin. "You could wear buckets and I'd still want you."

Extremely flattered and giving Josh side eye, Lisa jokes, "Buckets, that's giving me Nan vibes. Any issue there I should be worried about?"

"Jeez, aren't you a little fire cracker?"

Confidently Lisa comes into her own.
"You should see me explode Josh." Bites her lip. "You ever get that feeling you're drowning in someone? I'm that reservoir you'll wanna swim in, dive in."

Even Lisa is surprising herself with this confidence today and even makes a little purr noise, with a glint in her eye as they lock eyes, they both know, at this moment, she has him, has control - hook, line & sinker. Continuing to flirt with Josh.
"Rest your head down sweetheart, I need a seat."

Josh pulls out a pair of small florescent orange crotchless, fluffy knickers and passes them to Lisa, who goes pale and almost faints at such a ghastly garment.

Pauline goes to get in her Range Rover and the word "Slag" has been keyed onto the side of it. Pauline looks around, sees no one, but her eyes are fixated on Belinda's apartment and sees the curtain move. Pauline rings someone whom she never introduces to anyone and has on her phone as 'fireman Sam'.

"Hey babe, I need a huge favour. That Belinda is setting up on my street, number 58. Flush her out, good man."

Pauline hangs up the phone abruptly and with head held high, slides into her car and drives off extremely slowly, in a bid to let Belinda see her.

Pauline turns up the music full blast of *Blondie's* single '*One way or another.*'

Through cackling like a witch on purpose, Pauline sings her heart out.

"One way or another, I'm gonna getcha, getcha, getcha, one way or another."

Slight wheel spin when hitting the corner and going out of view. Belinda's curtains twitch.

Pauline does her usual visit to a sexual health clinic and is waiting to be seen in a basic beige waiting room with posters of HIV and Gonorrhoea all around, and one Vogue magazine on the wobbly table.

Rowdy couple, covered in love bites, sat waiting and kissing and making a slurping song no one wants to hear, especially Pauline, who huffs at the sound they are making.

Natalie is in her 20s, natural blonde hair back in a ponytail, long polished red nails, big brown eyes, feisty with a sarcastic mouth, is practically sat on her partner, Mark. With his large frame he looks intimidating to most, doesn't smile and looks like he wants to fight the world. Natalie decides to pipe up.

"You got a problem love?"

"You will have in a minute if you don't stop dribbling all over him, LOVE."

"Really? Bet you're here because you're riddled."

"I'm here to collect rubbers and lube for my working girls so we don't get riddled, unlike yourself. Here for a vagina swab?"

"Who the fuck do you think you are?"

"Madame Pauline to you. I'm practically royalty in this city."

"And I'm the queen - take a bow."

"Queen of the STD's. I like your mouth. Here's a card if you fancy making money with it, instead of wasting it on him."

"Ooii, mouth almighty, I love her."

"Of course you do, that's why you were at the Parlour thursday evening eh?"

"What?" Natalie fires up. "Skittles Thursday evening you said. I knew you were lying, something was off and you told me it was all in my head. You're always up for it, not that night, now I know why - you shagged one of her whores."

"Working girl would be a more appropriate name, thank you."

"God, I'm sorry. Mark, how could you?"

"This is bullshit, she's winding you up. It must have been someone who looks like me."

Pauline grins and squints her eyes. "Oh please. An Elvis tattoo on top right arm? Wearing Manchester United vest, which is too small for you by the way. I don't miss a trick."

Natalie gasps, Mark death stares Pauline as she holds up her little finger and wiggles it at him. Doctor calls out Pauline's name. "Bye babe." Pauline says through an exaggerated pout. Then ups her catwalk energy and struts off, leaving the couple arguing in the distance whilst she calmly walks into the doctor's office. Pauline looks back and winks at Mark, as she slowly pushes the door closed.

When returning from the clinic and shopping, Pauline turns into her street and sees a huge commotion; people, fire engines and police. A fire broke out, whilst Pauline was busy, at Belinda's place, now just simmering down. Pauline shrugs her shoulders and mutters to herself, "Oh well, never mind." She pulls up outside of her Parlour as a girl in a wheelchair pulls up next to her.

Maddie is 20, curly brown hair, dressed all in pink adidas tracksuit, glasses, brash, cute, and very confident.

"Beep, beep, excuse me, are you the owner of this place?"

"Sure am, I'm Pauline. Looking for someone?"

"Yeah, you. I need some work. I can't survive on my pitiful benefits money. I'm Maddie. Mad as hatter, some might say."

"Why are you in that chair Maddie? If you don't mind me asking."

"Paralysed from the waist down, so can't feel anything, which means I can go for hours and make you loads of money."

"Unless you've got a portable outside stairlift and a ramp, you'll not be able to get down there I'm afraid."

"I've got tons of experience and my dad can lift me down and back up for each shift, or a slave, they love that shit."

"And you think he won't cotton on that this is a sex Parlour with my big neon sign."

"He's paid for sex since my mum died, several times. He was driving the car that killed her and put me in this contraption, so he owes me." Winks at Pauline.

"Just when I thought I'd heard it all - Christ almighty. I've got a lot on my plate but have my number on this card, call me tomorrow. I can't promise anything"

"Aww, cheers Pauline. That's so cool."

Maddie swipes the card, fist pumps the air and wheels off down the road singing 'Spice up your life'.

Belinda, wide-eyed and steaming, sees Pauline and storms towards her. "I knew you'd stoop to an all-time low."

"What are you waffling on about?"

"Someone threw a bottle full of lit petrol through my window. I've just lost half my belongings, before I'd even moved in."

Pauline looks around all innocently.

"Oh I didn't see the fire engine. I only deal in diesel anyway. Just got back from the clinic."

Pauline pulls out some rubbers and lube.

"Here - want some?"

"Drop dead Pauline, this reeks of you. This has your hallmark all over it."

"You seem a bit unstable, a bit angsty - it's giving me rugby man energy. With what you've got left you can set yourself up in a little studio flat somewhere? All is not lost, surely?"

"This isn't the last you'll see of me. I'll point the police towards you."

"Good luck with that. I've been out, point them somewhere closer to home."

"Like?"

"You've got many enemies around here, take your pick."

"What is it with you? You just can't let the past go can you? After all these years."

"You ruined a relationship for me in the worst way possible and I will never forget it. You should have stayed in London, left me to move here on my own."

"I made one fucking mistake, when I was out of it on southern comfort and LSD, years ago."

"Betrayal has no time frame, the emotion attached to that will never die. Revealing my past to a man I was falling for and the repercussions of your mouth."

Pauline points her finger to Belinda's lips and presses down.

"This gob needs sewing up. Stay away from my life, my business and this street."

Belinda is tense and slightly trembling. "Piss off."

Pauline turns to walk away. "Bye honey bun."

"It's Belinda."

"I thought it was Barry."

"Don't start a fucking war with me - PAUL."

The rage in Pauline rises in an instant, turns around and lunges towards Belinda.

"The conflict has begun."
Pauline punches Belinda in the side of her head, with full force. She falls to pavement and cracks her nose.
"Next time I won't let you get back up."
Pauline pulls her wig off and throws it into the street.
Belinda, with a bald head, gets up, picks her wig up and puts it back on, but wonky to one side.

"Watch your back bitch."

Pauline tilts her head over her shoulder to look at her own back.
"Nope, nothing happening. You look like Les Dawson with that hideous wig." For one last dig - "Let me know where you set up next and I'll buy you an extinguisher and fire blanket - just in case."
Pauline walks off down the steps to her Parlour, as Belinda stood frozen, not knowing what to say.

Pauline walks through the Parlour, singing 'Disco Inferno' and approaches the girls, apart from Layla, in the lounge.

"Here we go girls, rubbers and lube from the lovely Doctor, he may pop in later on his way home. Got some stunning chocolate and mint ones. Lisa, I know you've got a sweet tooth."
Lisa blushes.
Pauline walks back through to put the stock away and out of one bedroom door comes Layla, with dilated pupils and trying not to show she is high, walks towards Pauline in a wobbly fashion and pleads to Pauline.

"I can't do him."

"Because you're too bloody high?"

"No, I just don't feel up to it. I'm tired"

"This isn't a pick and choose Parlour Layla. Get in there and earn your way."

"He wants to use cucumber on me."

"Be thankful it's not a marrow, now get back in there."

"I'm Pregnant."

"Bullshit. You wouldn't do coke if you were. And what I've seen you shove up your snout lately, I doubt it would survive one week in that toxic womb of yours."

Failed attempt to look innocent and win Pauline over; "Me?"

"I saw you earlier, so don't lie to me young lady, I'm not in the mood." Snaps Pauline, as she pushes Layla into the doorway, back into bedroom, and walks off just as the front door swings open and in walks Sandra, for the late shift, and new girl Leigh.

Pauline greets them with a smile. "Hello ladies, come on through to the back courtyard and have a G & T."

Leigh is 28, with a strong northern accent, tattoos, piercings, ripped jeans and 7" pink stilettos, brought along as an introduction from her mate Sandra, who has worked for Pauline for quite a few years, on and off. Sandra is 35, loud, husky voice, pocket rocket, pink hair scraped back too tightly, above her station, been on the game since she was 16.

"Heard so much about you Leigh." Opens Pauline.

"All good I bet."

"Not really, no. Quite the opposite in fact. But I like to make my own judgement calls."

"Good to know."

"Leigh short for Leighanna?"

"Yep, but I hate it, so I only like being called Leigh."

Sandra is upbeat and very enthusiastic about her mate working with her. There's tension between the girls, they all have gripes with Sandra, for separate reasons, and have all heard rough tales about Leigh. So Sandra is acting fearless and more forthright than usual, because Leigh is with her. "Come on Leigh let's have a drink and a fag before I show you the hottest whore house in the UK." Sandra says with volume.

"Alright girls." Leigh says to all as they walk through the lounge.

"Alright Leigh." They mutter in unison, Sheila looks down. Leigh walks out back with Sandra and Pauline and quickly sends a text which reads: "Yeah, she's here."

As the sun beats down over the courtyard, which is small, with high walls, trellis and roses up the walls, wind chimes, fairy lights and a bucket for cigarette ends, chats are in full swing and a party atmosphere. After having already had a few drinks, Pauline stares into Leigh's eyes, as Leigh is pouring herself a drink without asking.
"That'll be the last time you ever take anything of mine without asking. Clear?" Snaps Pauline.

"Shit, sorry, I wasn't thinking."

"How many hours you looking for? I'm not after part-time tarts, I want this place to start running at a 24-hour pace."

"As many as possible, I'm skint. Any chance of an advance?"

"I'm not a loan shark sweetheart, nice try though. When you've made some money then you'll be paid. Until then, drop your attitude and you can start tonight."

Leigh bites the side of her mouth to stop herself mouthing off. "Sound, cheers Doll."

"It's Pauline to you."

Phone rings in background and Lisa answers it. "Hello Polly's Parlour. Yes, Pauuulliinnneee it's for you."

Pauline walks to reception and takes phone "Hello."

"Hi. It's me from the clinic earlier, Natalie"

"Oh, queen gob-shite, that didn't take long."

"Had no choice did I? Thanks for the heads up by the way, I owe you one. I knew Mark was a snake deep down."

"Hurts when you realise you've been giving it away for free doesn't it?"

"Sure does. I'm now without a place to kip. Can I come see you for a chat?"

"Yes, you..." Pauline stumbles on her words as she gets a gut feeling something is not right, she slowly walks towards the bedroom door, which is slightly open, and can hear banging. Pauline pushes the door totally open. "...you can, just, one moment."

Pauline keeps phone in her hand and enters to see the window wide open and flapping with the evening breeze. Layla is led out on the bed covered in blood and not moving. Pauline drops the phone, is startled, leans against the wall, eyes glazed, and slides down the wall in shock.

CHAPTER TWO

Pebbles

Two days later, feeling exhausted from talking to the police, being at hospital worrying about Layla, and seeing Gary, who's been odd with her, Pauline is sat at Layla's bedside in Hospital. Layla is half awake, drowsy eyes, with marks all over her. Pauline looks at her with a tear in her eye.

"I'm so sorry this has happened to you. I will track this mother fucker down and when I do I'll kill..."

A female nurse enters the room, hearing the tail end of this conversation and looks at Pauline with a judgemental, raised eyebrow, up & down body scan. Disturbing the conversation, like a Matron from the 1940s.

"Morning. Layla, the results from the second scan reveal no internal damage but heavy bruising. You will need to rest and heal, your body has taken quite a traumatic blow. Pauline, the police are at reception and would like to speak to you."

"Thanks Auxiliary Nurse Julie."

Pauline makes sure Nurse Julie sees her look at her name badge. "Layla I'll see you tomorrow, get some more sleep." Pauline leans in to whisper - "Don't let Florence Nightingale fob you off with Paracetamol, aim for the top-notch stuff. You'll need it with your resilience - tenfold."

Layla cracks a slight smile. "Thanks Momma Polly."

Pauline kisses Layla on her forehead and leaves with a parting comment for nurse Julie.

"Opioids. That's what she needs, pronto." Pauline clicks her fingers at her. "Quick quick Julie."

Pauline walks towards two male policemen, biting the side of her mouth, with a cold look in her eyes. Pauline clearly has an issue with the law.

"Yes, how can I help?"

"Hello Mrs Cochran. We need to get access to a small camera in the corner of the outside shed by your front door?"

"It's a dummy."

"That's a shame. May be wise to step up security so you can keep the girls safe, in light of what's happened."

"You lot are a fine example of crap protection, everyone knows you all stay clear of the adult entertainment spaces, too scared of the temptation. Must be hard to help women who are sexually attractive. We are like vixens you want to explore, your heart pumps blood of sheer excitement, but you're too frightened you won't satisfy us, which you probably wouldn't. I will *always* look out for my girls. Besides, that cow upstairs from me probably has more of a spying eye than any camera, ask her. Now if you'll excuse me I have to get home now you've finished at mine."

A straight-faced, old school policeman, reacts dead pan to her little outburst and continues his thought out, preempted meeting with Brighton's tough talking Madame.

"We have followed all lines of inquiry with everyone, but unfortunately no luck just yet, but it's early days. Are you available now Mrs Cochran? We would like to speak to you again at the station."

Sarcastically responding to him.

"No problem at all officer, badge number BN256, I just need to go and get myself together and then I will join you in the luxury suite at the station. Get some real coffee in, not that cheap crap. I'll see you soon boys."

"We would rather you come now, there's just a couple of things to iron out, won't take long."

"Tough tits. I've not slept and I need to wash and change my clothes, so I'll be there as soon as I can. Take it or leave it."

"No problem, make it snappy though."

Pauline puts her middle finger up. "Snap this."

Policeman rolls his eyes as Pauline walks off, clanking her high heels down the corridor and shaking her behind because she knows they will be looking.

As Pauline arrives at her Parlour and walks towards her apartment, a terracotta plant pot smashes at her feet, dirt splashes up her legs.

Pauline looks up to see her neighbour, Nicki, with a grin on her face.

"OOOPPS, Sorry."

"You fucking will be."

"I hear Layla got a beating. About time this place got shut down."

"Surprised you didn't see anything suspicious, considering all you do is perch in that window like you're the president of neighbourhood watch."

"I don't get involved in police matters."

Pauline picks up part of the broken pot and flings it up at Nicki, who ducks, but it hits the window and cracks the glass.

"OOOPPS, sorry. Next time it'll be your throat."

Nicki looks shocked as Pauline makes a slit throat gesture and walks into her Parlour, as though it was a normal day for her.

Pauline walks around the apartment and thinks, deep in thought, in silence, with a vacant look in her eyes. The phone rings and snaps her out of the thinking process.

"Hello, Polly's Parlour. Yes, we are open later from noon. Thank you Mr Mason, see you at noon on the dot then, be lovely to see you again. Bye dear."
Pauline rings Natalie.
"Hi Natalie, you still want to work for me? Get glam and make your way here now. You'll be working until late so do whatever you need to do to stay awake and alert, as long as it isn't drugs. See you later."

A noise of a key fiddling with the lock at front door makes Pauline on edge, so storms towards the door with her heckles up. Door flings open - it's Sheila.

"For fuck's sake Sheila."

"Sorry. I left you a voicemail to say I can work today, didn't you get it?"

"No, I've been at Layla's bedside. I've got to go to the station in a minute. New girl Natalie be here soon, show her the ropes and keep an eye on everything for me. Ring Sandra and Leigh, I want you all working today, I've lost money due to the scum who attacked Layla. Lisa is on her way in."

"Right, I'll get on it."

"Can you pop up to that shop on the corner and ask Mike to install a camera for me, so we can monitor who comes to the door, need to make this place tight. Mike knows me, tell him to install today and set it up and let's crack on with business. Tell him I'll settle later, he will be fine about it."

"Will do. Have they found who hurt Layla?"

"Not yet, they will though, it'll all come to light. I'll tighten up security with the camera and I'll have a security guard here ASAP."

Pauline enters her bedroom and undresses, sprays fem fresh

below, puts fresh knickers on, sprays perfume, clean denim mini skirt, and a crisp white v-neck top, with cleavage showing, picks up the phone to make a call.

"Hello Andy, you still able to be my security? Yes, tonight at 8. Bless you mate, see you later. I'll get one of the girls to give you a free blow job at the end of your shift."

Pauline rushes out of the door and whispers goodbye to Sheila who's on the phone to Sandra.

"So you and Leigh will be in? I know, I've been worried too, but she is buying a camera for the door and we will have a security guard here at nights from now on. See you both in a bit."

Sheila puts phone down and shoves a lollipop into her mouth.

Pauline arrives at the police station and parks awkwardly, in the disabled bay. A young police officer, walking out of the station, tells her she can't park there.

"Arrest me if it bothers you that much young lad. I doubt you'll be getting any convicts in a wheelchair arriving whilst I'm here visiting, sunshine."

Policeman shakes his head and carries on walking.

Pauline walks in and is greeted by two different officers from whom she met at the hospital. One female, in her 30's, short hair, serious look on her face, dressed in grey trousers, waistcoat and white shirt with a male, late 40's, pot-belly, bald head, in an oversized, cheap, navy blue, polyester suit.

Pauline recognises him and he recognises her, but no words spoken.

After all the fannying around; shuffling papers, informal chat, reminding her she's not under arrest, just a routine interview, PC Polyester opens the conversation.

"Pauline, take me back to the attack. You took a call and saw the bedroom door open, then you entered. Take me through it, what did you see exactly?"

Pauline cringing and not falling for his display of authoritarianism.

Suddenly she recalls how she knows him, but keeps it under wraps.

"Like I said, Graham, I heard a noise, so I walked in and saw the window open. Layla on the bed covered in blood, so I called the police and ambulance. It's that basic. There isn't a revealing tale to tell, so no matter how many times you ask me, and in as many ways as you can - there is only one answer, and I have given you that, several times."

"Nothing else springs to mind? Anyone suspicious or left on bad terms recently? There's no record in your appointment book of anyone booked in with "Shakira," otherwise known by her real name, Layla, at that time?"

"That's right, some punters just turn up, so he must have done, as none of us saw anyone or booked anyone in, just a random fuck." Pauline winks at policeman. "You should know how it all works babe. Men just call in on the off chance don't they?"

Policeman looks uncomfortable and nervously grins at his colleague.

"HMRC aware of your income?" The cocky female officer chips in.

"Listen up, K.D Lang lookalike, I probably earn more than you in my sleep. I pay my taxes, so let's not go there." Pauline glares at the male policeman. "Wouldn't want anyone getting in trouble now would we? Everything is above board and I look after my girls."

Policeman sweating. "Pauline we..."

"Please, do call me Polly, Graham."

This second calling of his name is now obvious to his colleague that Pauline knows him and he's going pale with the thought Pauline may blow his cover any second.

"Any idea who could have a vendetta against you or the girls?"

Remembering he visited the Parlour several months previously, Pauline feels she has one over on him but keeping the information to herself.

"None at all. I've always maintained a high standard and never upset any punters. Maybe it was you? I just know you from somewhere and I can't quite put my finger on it. I'm sure it'll come to me."

As he quickly glances at her breasts and Pauline sees his eye-line drop, he becomes more agitated. "I am sure I would remember if we had met. Upset anyone outside of work? Anyone in your life who could be a suspect?" He goes on, nervously.

Pauline abruptly responds, because she never wants the police knowing her business. "Nope, keep myself to myself."

"How was Layla that day?"

"Fine. Raring to go and make money, as always."

"Nothing untoward? No worries?"

"Listen. She takes coke and she parties all the time. I'm not saying she's toxic, it's just, she's a danger to herself. Could be someone she knows or has pissed off, who knows." The interview techniques Pauline can see through, so in defiance at their boring repetitive questions, starts using "no comment" as it lingers a while and gets nowhere. PC Polyester concludes the interview and Pauline goes out to her car, with a deep sigh of relief.

Whilst thinking she has a flashback of the morning she left Gary's house. Gary, 35, muscle man, covered in tattoos, gold thick jewellery, thick set neck, white teeth, tight t-shirt, bling watch, with piercing blue, cheeky eyes. Gary grabs her tightly and whispers, "You're mine now."

Pauline nervously replies, "See you later babe."

Pauline jerks out of the flashback memory and shudders, pulls out mobile and calls Lisa.

"Hello Polly's Parlour."

"Lisa, it's me, can you meet? Surfer's Cafe on seafront, need to speak to you. Be there in 15."

Lisa and Pauline are comfy at the seafront cafe, with rustic wooden tables and colourful art work on the walls, mostly of sunsets and surfers riding the waves, sitting together in the window seat on cushions, sipping hot chocolate.

"Lisa, I'm shitting myself."

"Why? I've never seen you like this before. What's wrong?"

"I've lied to the police. They asked if I was seeing anyone and I said no. I couldn't mention gangster Gary because..."

"Because?"

"I've heard stuff about him but you know what I'm like; I love a bit of rough, it's a turn on and I turn a blind eye to what people get up to. But it's all falling into place, things I've overheard or been told in the past. The mere mention of his name to the cops and..." Pauline zones out.

"And what? Polly?"

"They would be all over him and I'd need a new identity. He does not like trouble at this door or he flips. He's involved in too much"

"Bloody hell Polly."

"I know, this is why I wanted to call it off. Some of what Tania told me about him came flooding back. What the hell have I got myself involved in? He's heavily into me and sees me as his, but I've heard what he's like if a woman rejects him. It's felt weird between us the past couple of days, like a coldness. I could feel there's some kind of shift, as if he knows something. I am good at picking up on energy aren't I? It's giving me shivers just talking about it. I've got all that hanging over me stressing me out, and now what's happened to Layla."

"Can't you talk to him and tell him the truth?"

"He beat Tania to a pulp just for talking to someone behind his back, imagine if he knows I run a 'Hooker Home' and have sex for money."

Pauline goes into deep thought, looking vulnerable and sad, rarely seen by anyone, ever.

"You don't think this is all connected do you?"

"What?"

"Him, then Layla being attacked?"

"I pray not, but I never saw who came in. When I spoke to her in the hallway she was definitely high and not her normal self. She was off her face. I was in the midst of meeting new girl, Gary on my mind, I just pushed her back to the door and walked off and told her to get on with it. I feel so sad I did that. I don't know what to think."

"Ok, let's think of something."

"Bless you love, it's too deep for you. Thank you for being there for me, you're one of the few people I can trust, but I need to sort this. Make your way to work darling and I'll have a walk and clear my head."

"Ok. I'll see you at work."

Lisa gives Pauline a tight hug, like a daughter to her mother. Both walk off in a different direction. Pauline walks along the pebbles, under grey clouds and looks out at the rough sea and takes a few breaths in, sits down on the pebbles, in a spot where there is no one around.

Back at Polly's Parlour Lisa walks through the door to hear cheering and laughing. She enters the lounge to see Sheila, Leigh and Sandra welcoming Natalie to the gang with bubbly.

"Wow, really? Layla is in hospital and Pauline has loads to deal with and you are all partying."

Leigh speaks as though she's been working there for years. "What's our pretty Polly got on her plate?"

"Errmm, well, Layla for starters."

Sandra decides to join in. "And what Lisa? Come on, teachers pet, you know something don't you?"

"No, get stuffed Sandra and stop showing off in front of your new mate."

"We've known each other for ages actually." Leigh declares.

Lisa totally unimpressed and throws a dirty look. "Pffftt. Sheila wanna come shop with me? We need to get wet wipes and oils?"

"Yeah sure. Let me put my buffalo boots on."

"Yeah run along Sheila, like you always do." says Sandra.

Sheila, usually timid, raises her voice, unexpectedly. "What the fuck are you chatting about?"

Sandra changes topic, partly shook. "Nothing. Say hello to Natalie then Lisa."

"Welcome Natalie, I'll catch up with you when I'm back. Won't be long." Lisa and Sheila walk out of the flat. As Lisa and Sheila walk up the road they are unaware they're being watched by a man, in a white van.

"Sheila, I need to tell you something. Promise me you won't say anything."

"Guides honour."

"Like you were ever in the Girl Guides."

"Well, no, but I've got the outfit, for work."

"Jesus! Right, it's about Polly - she's in trouble."

"What kind of trouble?"

"I just spoke with her, the fear in her eyes upset me. She's in heavy with that Gary geezer, but I'm not sure of the whole story, nor is she, by what I could make out."

"I've heard he's violent and done time in jail."

"What? Does Polly know?"

"She knows he's done time for GBH and other fights, but he did time for rape, which I am not sure she knows about." I only heard that earlier today, from that Morgan, you know the one who works in sun-bed shop. I didn't want to burst Polly's bubble, and it's not solid facts, she's a bit of a storyteller that Morgan. Polly seems so happy lately too, I want her to be happy. Where is she now?"

"What the hell, we need to tell her. Maybe Morgan got it twisted,

I know her quite well, but she's known as the gossip queen. Let's get these bits for work then ring her, she's down on seafront getting some fresh air."

Sheila and Lisa walk into a pound shop, hand in hand.

Down on the beach there's a slight drizzle of rain, but Pauline loves this on her face and enjoys sitting on her own in peace.

Pauline is smoking a cigarette, looking out at the wild sea and daydreaming, watching the waves, in her own little world.

Gary appears from behind, creeps up slowly to grab her by the waist.

"Oooiii, oooiiiii."

"Christ Gary, bloody hell. How did you know I was here?"

"Tah dahhhh!"

Pauline is trying to conceal her stress by his sudden arrival.

"Nice to see you, but how did you know I was here?"

"Don't you worry about me, cupcake, I'm all over this city like a rash. I always know where my lady will be, at all times. I've got your back, come here."

Gary pulls Pauline tightly to him and hugs her, overly tight to make her know something is wrong. His grip on her hips is brutal. The look on Pauline's face is a fake smile, uneasy look in her eyes, not knowing how to react.

"How about we go somewhere nice and cosy? Relax together, maybe with some oils perhaps?"

"Like where?"

"Umm, I don't know. How about somewhere cheap and cheerful like...Polly's Parlour?"

Gary grabs her by the wrist.

"One fucking squeal out of you and I'll drag you out to sea and that'll be your final resting place."

"Gary, please, honestly, it's not what you think. I'm just..."

Gary grabs the back of her hair and pulls her to the sea and trips her up, face into water. Pauline gasps for air and pleads with him to stop.

"I can't hear you, 'Polly'."

Gary lifts her up and pushes her back down onto the pebbles.

"Please, Gary, let me explain."

"Try me."

"Years ago I ran away to London because..."

"Oh here comes the sob story."

"You know part of my life story, I told you when we met. I'm now trying to tell you what brought me to this lifestyle as I got older."

Gary starts to quietly laugh in a sinister style and throws pebbles at her legs. "Awww poor little Polly. I know some of the story, but you missed out one tiny little detail didn't you."

"Honestly - please. What are you doing? That's hurting me. I'm trying to be truthful, I was planning on telling you, honestly, ask Lisa."

"You what? Talking about me to other hookers? Making me out to be a mug."

Gary grabs a big pebble and throws it at her crotch. "Bet you've had bigger up there, haven't you? That pussy paid for, you dirty slag. I now know - you're a fucking man"

"No, I am not a man, never ever saw myself as one either. Please stop throwing those, you're frightening me babe."

"I'm not your babe, you belong to all the perverse fuckers of this world, banging that pussy for money. How about I get a freebie eh?"

Gary kneels down and looks around at how empty it is, then puts his hand up her skirt and rips her knickers down as she starts to cry and tries to fight back, but Gary is brutal and far too powerful, with the look of a serial killer in his eyes

"I will ruin you, and your tranny cunt."

Gary places his hand over her mouth then undoes his jeans zip and has his way with her. Fast motion sex, like she is nothing, pounding her harder than she's ever experienced, with the look of terror on her face, in tears, which seems to turn him on even more, as he groans and smiles and finishes within a couple of minutes.

When he pulls away he does his zip up and throws a five pound note at her.

"Keep the change 'Prozzy Polly' - get yourself a sweet tea on your way home, should help you with the shock."

Gary whistles 'hit me baby one more time', and walks off with his head in the air and lights a spliff. Pauline curls up into ball, in shock, and closes her eyes.

Lisa and Sheila have bought goodies for the Parlour and are walking back when Lisa rings Pauline to check in on her.

"Hi, you ok to talk?"

"I, um, help me Lisa."

"Polly what's wrong, where are you?"

Through gritted teeth. "I'm just down the seafront."

"I've got Sheila with me, we're on our way."

Lisa puts phone down before Pauline could answer. Lisa and Sheila run as fast as they can towards the seafront and spot Pauline stumbling away from the sea, towards the promenade.

"Oh my god Polly, what's happened? You're bleeding."

"Give me those wet wipes." Pauline sits down, takes the wipes out of Lisa's hands and wipes herself clean, composes herself and wipes the running mascara off of her face. "Not a word to anyone about this ok?"

"You've not told us what's happened? Is this to do with that bloody Gary?" Lisa asks.

"Now, listen to me girls, you saw nothing. We move on and we go to work, that's how we survive. I don't want to discuss it. Keep your lips tight shut ok? For your own safety, trust me."

With tears in her eyes, Sheila responds. "I know that look Polly, I promise you I will not tell a soul."

"Thank you girls. Sheila can you make your way back and if anyone asks I am with Lisa doing lunch and we will be up soon. I just need to sit here for a while."

"Of course, yes. If you need anything you let me know won't you?" Sheila kisses Pauline on the cheek and gives her a side embrace but Pauline is too stiff to respond.

Sheila heads off up a back street and puts her headphones on.

Pauline takes Lisa's hand. "Lisa, you know when I was talking to you the other day but we cut it short, well I feared he may have been asking around about me, as he's too paranoid, too much coke I suspect. I ignored my gut feeling and I'm kicking myself for it, because he now knows about the Parlour."

"I'm furious Pauline, you don't deserve to be treated like this by anyone. He's done time for rape and..."

"WHAT?"

"I found out literally half an hour ago Polly. Sheila told me and that's why we rang you as she was told this morning but didn't want to say anything. Did he? To you?"

"Yes. Never in all my life as a working girl have I felt so violated."

"What can we do?"

"Trust me darling, his turn will come."

"What kind of revenge are we talking about here?"

"It's best I keep this one to myself. Let Momma Polly sort this alone. Not a word ok?"

"Promise."

Pauline drifts off in her head whilst still looking at Lisa. "He knows."

Lisa is one of only a few people in her life that she shares everything with.

"Oh shit."

Lisa puts her arm around Pauline and Pauline rests her head on Lisa's shoulder as they sit in silence looking out at the sea.

Sheila is briskly walking back, past parked cars and a van side door opens and someone pulls Sheila in from behind. Robert has slicked back wet look hair, neck tattoos, missing front tooth, quite a handsome man, in his 30's, wearing a white vest and tight pale blue jeans. Robert pins Sheila to the floor inside the van and puts a hand over her mouth.
"Well, well, well, if it isn't saucy Sheila. How are you sweetheart?" says Robert as he laughs. "Why did you run away?"

Sheila, with a stare in her eyes of absolute shock, but also a bit happy to see him, tries to speak. Robert relaxes his hand from her mouth, so she can speak.
Quick thinking Sheila spins a tale. "I didn't run from you, I ran from someone who raped me, he made me do it. He forced me to come down here and I was petrified."
"What? You could have run to me, not all the way down south."
"He said he was watching you and if I told he would slit your throat, so I wanted to save you Robert, I swear on my..."
"Who is he? Where is he?"
"Gary. He lives around here, but he's evil."
Robert sits back and lets Sheila catch her breath to think for a minute. "I want the whole story, start to finish."
"So two weeks before I ran..." Sheila goes off on a tangent with a long story; part true, part made up. Sheila had run from Robert, because she had slept with his rival and she was scared of what may happen, so came south to start a fresh, even though she liked Robert a lot. He was her pimp, and boyfriend, but she wanted independence and more money, so was brave to pick a place on the map and went alone, carving a little life out for herself.

Pauline and Lisa walk through the door of Polly's Parlour and Pauline heads straight into the shower, gets changed and is upbeat in front of the girls and acts as if nothing has happened. "Right, girls, let's look at the appointment book and see what's what. Sheila? Sheila?"

"She's not here, she went out with you Lisa." Says Leigh, matter of factly.

"Yeah, should be back by now though as she slipped off for a sun-bed, whilst me and Polly grabbed some food."

"Just had a guy on the phone wanting a threesome, so me and Leigh are going to do him." Sandra replies proudly. "Then Solider Shaun will be here in half an hour in his camouflage gear, he's asked for our lovely new girl, Natalie."

"Hey Nat, welcome." Pauline says, whilst smiling her way through this conversation.

"We will go through money etc later. It's throwing you in at the deep end with this one; he's 10 inches and bangs hard. You ok with that?"

Natalie trying to be cool and not nervous. "Fine by me, my dildo is 12" so..."

"Right, of course it is. Lisa, if you can sort the laundry, I'll make us a brew. Hop to it girls. Sandra gives Natalie a gallon of lube. Make sure you all smell nice and fresh for today's punters."

Sandra throws some shady comment; "As if we wouldn't ever be fresh. I always..."

Pauline loudly corrects Sandra mid-flow. "Not being funny Sandra, but gobble Gavin said it was a bit of a cringe minge the last time he dined out down there." Pointing to Sandra's crotch.

"WOW! No wonder he asked me for a discount. Why did he gob off at you about it? It's because it's not true, I am constantly using that flannel."

"Oh my God, not that Pink one on the side?" Leigh replies with a screwed up face.

"Yeah that's mine."

"I washed my fucking face with that earlier, why didn't you tell me?"

"You're the new girl on the block around here, you'll learn quickly enough to use your own things and no one else's."

"I could catch something."

"Are you kidding? You did bareback yesterday for an extra thirty quid. And you're moaning about my M & S flannel."

Pauline has zoned out and has a flashback in her head of the beach and suddenly changes her whole demeanour.

"STOP FUCKING BICKERING AND GET TO WORK. And you Sandra, have a shower, not a flimsy flannel wash. I don't want this place getting a reputation for your vile vagina, now piss off, the lot of you."

All girls fall silent and can see in Pauline's eyes that she means business and not to fuck with her in this moment.

Lisa breaks the atmosphere. "OK, I'm going to ring Sheila."

Pauline walks into kitchen, holds onto the side, bows her head and takes a deep breath as she flicks the kettle on.

Sheila has finished telling her tale to Robert, then he proceeds to give her a huge hug and a kiss on the lips. Sheila's phone rings, Robert puts his hand over it.

"Don't answer it. I've spent all this time looking for you and the whole time you've been frightened. You're my girl, and always will be. You're coming back up North with me."

"I can't, not yet, we need to sort Gary out don't we, or else he will look for me and I'm scared Robert."

"Indeed we do. I only arrived this morning, so let's make a week of it and I will sort him out, don't you worry."

"You can stay at mine, it's just a small bedsit, but I need to see Polly first."

"Not without me at your side. I want to meet her, she sounds like she's been there for you. I'd like to thank her for looking after you for me."

"Things are different here; she's not like a pimp, we get good money here, she's my boss and I adore her. I have no intention of leaving, this is my new life. Robert, please, trust me - you can sit here and wait, there's no back exit to the flat, so I can't go anywhere. I don't need to run again. Not this time."

"Give me your phone to hold on to, that'll make me feel like you won't run." Robert shows he's insecure.

Sheila edgy but needs to get away and think. It's been 6 months since she saw him, her head is scrambled, so knows it's a good trade off, so she can be alone with Pauline and get some advice. Sheila is happy here, feeling free and made new friends. She's not feeling the fright enough to run.

"Of course, my sweet man, here, hold the phone. But I can promise you I will be back shortly." Sheila hands him her phone and kisses him and walks back into Polly's Parlour.

Back inside Sheila walks into the lounge.

"Here she is. What's the matter?" Pauline asks, due to Sheila's worried face.

"It's Robert. He's here."

"Who?"

"Oh wow, he's never come from up north? Sheila he's always told people he likes you a lot. Where is he?" Says Leigh.

"Outside, but I've just lied really badly to him."

Pauline takes Sheila's arm. "Right young lady, look at me. If you had to lie for your safety or because you felt that was the only thing you could do, then fuck it, men lie all the time. Did he believe you? Need me to speak to him?"

"He did say he'd like to meet you but..."

Pauline fiercely walks away and does not let Sheila finish her sentence and is yelling out as she walks.

"Which one is his car?"

"It's a white van, straight outside."

Pauline stomps up the concrete steps leading up from her door, like a woman possessed, and flings open Roberts passenger door.

"I take it you're Robert?"
Pauline gets in and slams the door shut.

Robert, normally an alpha male and takes no shit, is a little startled, but flirts a little, as this usually wins women over.
"And you must be the delightful Polly?"

"Save the charm lad, it doesn't connect with me. You aren't taking her away from me, let's get that clear. She's one of my top earners."

"So she's a cash machine to you?"

"Been around the block way too long sunshine. I protect what's mine. I run a tight ship with eyes on everything. Do you like her?"

Robert not been approached by a female so harshly as this before, so a bit lost for words.
"She's a cracking girl, and um, although a lot younger than me, there's something striking about her. I wouldn't have driven hundreds of miles if I didn't want her in my life."

"Good, then you'll not stand in the way of her new life. You wanna hang around, I can get you some security work on my door and at the weekly orgies I run, if she wants you to be here that is. Up for that?"

Robert shocked. "I, I, I came here to get her back up to Leeds with me. She's told me this is her new life and seems happy. She talks highly of you."

"If you want her to be happy you'll stay here, prove yourself. I will be observing, closely, always."

"I'm not sure, I need to think."

Pauline looks at him up close, right in the eyes, with total conviction, lowering her voice deep, making Robert blush.
"Hurry up and think, my offer expires tomorrow."
Pauline opens the door and gets out, looks back at him.
"Come on, follow me."

"Sure."

Robert follows like an uncertain lost puppy, totally at Pauline's powerful control, which she is radiating plentiful today.

The beach attack has notched her angsty vibe upwards and Robert has walked into her territory, at a time when NO-ONE will be dominating her in any way.

Pauline has more fire in her than ever before and those around her can feel it - it's a force everyone can feel from her energy alone.

Pauline starts walking towards the Parlour steps, Robert hastily following. Pauline catches a glimpse of Nicki peeping through the curtains and shouts out;

"YEAH, I CAN SEE YOU, NOSEY NICKI."

In a confrontational manner, Nicki opens the window. "You what? Hard to hear what you're saying with that 40 fags a day throat."

"Robert, this is Nicki. She's the best shit shag you'll ever meet, and a gob with no substance behind it. Dead behind the eyes, null and void."

"What the hell is your problem? I didn't do anything to you personally."

"You lost me money, end of. You became complacent with it, you didn't fulfil your duties as a working girl. How many times do I have to repeat myself, it's getting boring."

"How about a trial shift? I'll work it off for you."

"Aww, that's so sweet. NO."

Pauline and Robert walk down the steps cackling. Nicki has tears in her eyes, moves back in quickly, so no one sees her vulnerability.

Back inside the Parlour, Pauline storms in at a pace faster than usual.

"EVERYONE, this is Robert." She loudly announces.

"Sheila we've had a chat, you can go off and have a meal with him and talk things through, see what happens."

"It's all thanks to Leigh." Robert announces.

Pauline's attention turns to Leigh, very calmly walks up to her.
"So, Leigh -ANNA, you told him she was here?"
Pauline grabs her by the collar.
"Listen to me, darlin', you're lucky he's not come to cause trouble, if he had, you'd be out of here. You may have got into scraps out there on the streets, in here you're under my rules. You do not talk about the girls to anyone. Understood?"

Leigh, bright red in the face, but with a tiny bit of attitude;
"Yeah, alright. Loud & clear. Everyone knows he likes her, I thought I was helping that's all."

Sheila looks on confused.
"Sorry, Polly, can we talk in the office a minute please. Robert make yourself a cuppa, won't be long. Make him feel welcome girls."

Pauline and Sheila sit across the desk from each other in the small office. Pauline pours herself a large Brandy and swigs it back in one mouthful and warmly speaks to Sheila.
"You're a good kid, bright for your age. I can read men a mile off, trust me, he's into you, he's definitely into his feelings about you, I know that for a fact. I can feel it too, when he talks about you.
That doesn't mean I'm not weary, the jury is still out, let's just see what happens sweetheart. Have a meal, talk with him, see what you feel. Ring me if you need to bail."

"When he's moody he turns me on and scares me at the same time, don't know why. I always wonder why an older man would want me for nothing other than sex. How can a relationship work if the girl is selling sex as a job?"

Pauline rests her hand on her shoulder.
"It's just sex Sheila, you know that. There's no real attachment or emotional connection, it's like acting sex - it's a job.
If in your heart you don't feel violated, degraded or emotionally unstable, then it's not time to pack up the handcuffs and whips.
Have an evening together, forget about work for an evening, have a massive chocolate pudding."

Sheila bluntly, but also scared, blurts out;
"I told him Gary followed me from Leeds and raped me."

Pauline stands up. "You said? You mean? Gary my Gary?"

"I didn't know what he wanted from me, I felt guilty for leaving him, I was caught off guard, I had to think of something dramatic to make him believe I had valid reason to run. Shit, I'm so sorry Polly."

"It's fine, it's just, you know. Fuck, fuck, FUUUCK."

Both stare into each other's eyes and both well up with a tear and have a moment of connection, which Pauline rarely reveals about herself, but to her girls...they see it more often than anyone in the outside world.

"I've got your back Sheila."

"Like wise. Thanks, Polly, you're like the mother I never had."

"And you're like the daughter I never wanted."

Whilst both roaring with laughter Pauline holds Sheila's hand.
"Now get outta here before you start making those things appear again."

"What things?"

"Those teardrop things, I don't like them. Right, give me a hug, go and enjoy a meal."

Flippantly putting an end to what could make her more emotional, yet letting it be known she cares, and that sadness isn't worth dwelling on.

Times like these, Sheila has glimpses of a part of her, which is a warm and supportive figure, even when she is being stern there's a genuineness radiating from her.

There's a heart hiding underneath her fortress and when shown it's an honour for some. This is why people often refer to her as a 'tart with a heart'.

Sheila and Pauline walk towards the door, Pauline's arm around Sheila's shoulders.

Outside of Polly's Parlour can mostly be busy with people walking to and from the beach, shoppers using the stores at one end of the street, someone always selling the big issue and residents for the street itself and from the tower block opposite, adding to the colourful vibe, so there's always a 'foot fall' of clients. There are those on a whim, those who walk past daily and wish they had money, or to give it a go and not be found out, or the brave enough ones to cheat on their partners for a quickie, and those who want to lose their virginity.

Polly's Parlour has flower pots around the Polly's Parlour sign, the steps are always swept, the paint work has zero chips or dirt anywhere outside. All sorts visit; workmen on a lunch break, city slick suited professionals, young men after the clubs and pubs close. Everything from six-pack 20 years olds off their faces on drugs or drink, or both, to men in rain coats, with a support stocking, hearing aid and clearly over 80. If ever there were a prime location for the best brothel in the UK, Polly's Parlour is the one, the hub of this diverse community. Pauline has a nose for money too, it's like a sixth sense; she can smell it in the air the minute it leaves the royal mint and what wallet it will land in, and how much.

Polly's Parlour is her pride and joy and a business she is orchestrating wisely, to secure her future. Money is her driving force, to retire early with it is the plan.

One of these gentleman, a new customer, older, long black coat, briefcase, grey hair and thick glasses, was looking lost outside. When he sees the sign, he knocks on a flat door, looking for number 48a, but has knocked on Nicki's door, 48b, by accident. Nicki opens the door in just her dressing gown, in a foul mood.

"Yes? What do you want?"

"Hi, it's me, John, I rang this morning. Polly?"

Nicki hesitates, thinks for a second and changes her tone instantly.

"Oh, John, yes of course, hi, come on through. Sorry it's been hectic today, you're in the diary. Two hours was it?"

"Just the one dear, I can only take so much scat." He proudly states.

Nicki's face is a picture of hidden revulsion, but needs the money. This is the first time, since being kicked out of Polly's Parlour, that she's had a man who has knocked on the wrong door. In a flash of desperation Nicki's eyeballs turn into pound coins, and she runs with it.

"Yes, indeed, please, go on through to the bedroom and make yourself comfy. I'll be with you shortly."

Nicki runs to bathroom cabinet, in high anxiety, and scrambles with what she has. At the back she finds a box of laxative chocolate, and scoffs them in a hurry, the whole box.

Pauline puts the phone down after a conversation with the hospital and bellows out so all can hear, punters too.

"Good news everyone. Layla is getting better and more alert. Praise the Lord. I'm off to see her in a bit."

Pauline says goodbye to Sheila and Robert as they leave.

"You look after her, you hear me?"

Robert nods like a naughty school boy as they exit, he bows his head.

Pauline secretly loves this alpha position over him, it can be seen in a slight smirk at the side off her mouth, it's ultra slight, the human eye can barely grasp a peek at it before it retracts, but it means a huge deal to her. There's a celebration of tingling feelings going on behind Pauline's mask when she is in this position. She is, after all, a Madame, a business woman, feisty spirited and a mother figure to her girls, all rolled into one. She thrives better when she has control, especially over men. She knows she's earned the right to be savage and act cold when in defence mode, if a possible threat to heart and mind is presenting itself.

Those beautiful features are locked away in a vault, so anyone who can 'see' the real her, is a blessed human being. Pauline's reputation is admired, by most.

Pauline looks in the diary.

"Girls? Who booked in someone called John at 6pm?"

"That was you." Sandra hollers back.

"Oh balls, so I did, it's 6.45pm. That was for you Sandra."

"What was it for?"

Pauline was about to tell her but there's a gentle knock on the door. Pauline is right by the door, giving a hanging mirror a quick wipe over, so looks relieved, John no doubt. She steps forward to the door and opens it with a smile. Pauline's emotions are easily read at this moment; she is shocked, it's Gary.

CHAPTER THREE

Payback

Pauline is at door with Gary about to step in when he sees the camera light on the new camera, just inside the doorway. Gary changes his angry face to a kind, sweet, smiling face and casually takes Pauline's wrist and 'guides' her outside.

"Why haven't you replied to my text? A thank you would've been nice."

"Let go of my wrist, it's hurting."

Gary proceeds to mimic Pauline, in a childish voice.

"Let go of my wrist it's hurting. What the fuck is wrong with you, Polly?"

Upstairs Nicki is leaning out of the window, Gary and Pauline are unaware she can see and hear parts of the conversation, not all, due to the street noise drowning them out.

"After what you did to me on the beach, you think you can waltz in here and act like it's OK."

"We had sex and you got paid. Isn't that what you do for a living?"

"You forced yourself on me, that's jail time."

Gary pushes her up against the wall.

"Keep your fucking mouth shut or I'll go for round two. I don't want anyone knowing I've been fucking a tranny."

Nicki comes out of her apartment and coughs, on purpose, so they know she's there. Gary let's go of Pauline. They look up to see Nicki, who starts to speak to Pauline.

"Everything alright Polly?"

"Yep, all fine. Gary was just leaving."

Gary walks up the steps and spits near Nicki's feet, gets into his black BMW and lights a cigarette, but doesn't start the car. Nicki goes to the top of the steps and walks down the first couple to get closer, and looks down at Pauline.

"Who is he? I recognise him you know. I've seen him outside a couple of times. Dodgy punter?"

"He's nobody, trust me. When have you seen him?"

"Last time was the night Layla got hurt, he was across the road in that same car, I think. I'm sure it's him. The police have asked me twice if I have seen anything or anyone, but I don't want heavy shit at my door. But now I've seen how he was with you, I think we should tell the police."

"No, seriously Nicki, leave it. I can handle him."

"Really? Didn't look like it to me."

"Well, I can. It's nothing I can't sort out."

"I've got you, if you need me."

"Honestly, I'm alright."

Pauline goes back into her Parlour and leaves Nicki stood thinking. Gary starts car and pulls away. Nicki stares at him, they lock eyes, giving Nicki the creeps.

On the Seafront, Sheila and Robert are sitting outside a fish restaurant about to order. Sheila sees Gary at the traffic lights opposite and starts to shake, her eyes fixated on his car.

"What's the matter?"

"That's him, Gary, in the BMW."

"Have a couple drinks then order me the same meal as you, I will be back soon, sit tight babe."

"Please be careful, he's a nutter, please just..."

Robert speeds off to follow not allowing Sheila to finish her words, leaving her to order.

When he arrives at the other end of the city, after following Gary, Robert pulls over, a bit behind, and watches Gary unload a black bag from the boot of his car and walk into his house.

Pauline is in the third bedroom, which is hers and rarely gets used for punters. Pauline is lying on the bed, and has been deep in thought for ten minutes about numerous times she has been mistreated by men; punched her because she transitioned, treated her like a fuck toy and broken her heart.

When Pauline sits up, there's a fire in her belly, she's had enough, she's at boiling point - it's time to lean on someone for help, to deal with Gary.

The only person she can think of to call is Tania.

"I need your help Tania, are you around? Fantastic. Meet me at the end of the pier? Great. I'll meet you there in 10 minutes."

Leigh comes out of the bathroom totally dolled up; full make up, hair straightened, little black dress, diamond earrings and dainty necklace.

"Well Hellloooo, look at you. Girls come here, look, this is the kind of effort you should be making - pure class. Take note, step up your game girls. I'm off out so have a good time and I'll be back in a bit. Andy will be here to work the door shortly. Lisa, make him feel at home"

Pauline walks out in a hurry.

Shortly after, Lisa flicks through the diary as Leigh and Sandra walk into the lounge, Natalie follows them. Lisa answers the door to Andy.

Andy is ginger, 6ft 5, black jacket with 'Security' written on the back, black jeans and DM's, green eyes, warm smile. Lisa takes a bit of a shine to him instantly and smiles and flutters her eyelashes.

"Hey Andy, I'm Lisa, nice to meet you."

"Cheers Lisa. Nice to put a face to a name. Are you the one giving me my free blow job?"

Lisa bright red in the face. "Excuse me?"

"Polly said it was part of my payment for doing the door."

"Oh, that'll be one of the working girls, I'm just the receptionist."

Andy winks at her. "She said you'd say that."

Lisa is trying not to hide that her toes are curling and she is not down for that, but smiles nonetheless.

"I see. Come through to the lounge, I'll introduce you to the girls, take your pick later." Both walk off into the lounge.

Pauline is at the end of the Pier. It's 7.30pm, noisy, busy, bright and Pauline is waiting whilst eating candy floss and looking out at the full moon pouring its reflection onto the sea.

Someone grabs her waist and Pauline sharply turns around with her fist clenched, still holding candy floss and about to punch out, then notices it's who she's waiting for.

Julie is a very masculine lesbian, rings on every finger, has angst energy and is with Tania, who's alternative, bohemian, long curly auburn hair, feminine rose petal dress on and loads of hippy bangles on her wrists.

"You fucking... oh it's you."

All three laugh and Pauline hugs both affectionately. Tania can sense Pauline is off.

"Hey love, what's up? This must be quite serious, we've not seen you for Eons."

"I don't know where to start Tan."

"Let's sit on the beach."

"I can't sit down there at the moment. I just can't..." Pauline is upset and Tania knows this is not like her, puts her arm around

Pauline.

"Hey that's ok. What's upsetting your soul? I can feel your energy is off."

"Tania, I've got myself involved with Gary."

"Not gangster Gary?"

"Yes, him."

"What the...after all those things I told you about him?"

"I know, I know, but that was years ago, and we were doing lots of drugs back then. Some stuff happened recently and it clicked in my head that it was him."

"That asshole is due a good hiding." Julie angrily adds.

"That's why I rang you both. Julie, I know you've got it in for him and he's..." Pauline cries.

"He's raped me. And now I think he's attacked Layla."

"No, not Layla at your place?"

"She's in hospital Tan, beat up real bad. She's recovering well, but they've not found who did it."

"What the hell have you got entwined with? He drains the aura. Mate, I need to balance out your chakra's."

Julie jumps in. "Babe, fuck the chakra's for now eh? Polly, how did you get involved with that wanker?"

"I was at a low, my past creeping up, as it does. About a month ago I was drunk and in a bar."

Pauline describes that evening; double gins, Gary smiling at her whilst he's playing a fruit machine and smoking. He slides up beside her and turns on the charm and asks her what's wrong. Pauline talks about how her mum was recently on her death bed in hospital and Pauline wanted to be the adult and give her forgiveness. This she found terribly hard to do, but did go and see her. Before she passed away she had given her a letter, saying she had nothing left and even if she did she would have given it to a cat charity, rather than her and that she will always be one of life's failures, a hopeless romantic, looking in all the wrong places for love.

She also wrote that even after surgery she was never the daughter she would have wanted, this broke Pauline, but this part she kept out of the story for Gary.

So this night was a farewell drink and Gary praises her spirit, her outfit, her smile, and says he feels immensely drawn to her. Pauline was flattered by his compliments, she needed to hear this, it was a perfect time for a predator to pounce on his prey. Gary made a toast of a good riddance to her mother, this made her smile, which hooked her in.

"The right one comes along when you're not looking, so she's wrong about tonight - because I found you."

"I am very touched." Pauline admits. "That's very sweet, but I'm a lot older than you."

"With age comes wisdom and growth, that's all I want in a woman; someone with substance and meaning, not some young giggly girl. You have something about you. Let me buy you dinner tomorrow?" Gary had all the charm in his delivery.

Pauline looks at Julie and Tania.

"And that, my lovelies, is how I got reeled in. Full on, meals, days out, a posh weekend away, gifts and then...he found out about Polly's Parlour and my past."

"Shit, Polly. You know he did time for a rape charge years ago? I only heard that recently. His past is dark."

"I found that out just after he...he..." Pauline fighting back the tears. "That mother fucker got me down there on the beach, in broad FUCKING daylight."

Julie livid at this news. "Pauline, he can't get away with this. How many more are out there that he's hurting? He needs to be stopped."

"I knew you'd understand why I've called you guys - I want him done over."

"Whoah, what? That's not what I had in mind to be honest. I thought get him done by the police and he will go away again for years, or a nice beating, or both."

Tania and Pauline in unison - "NO WAY."

"You're not both suggesting we bump him off?"

"The best way I'd say. I won't ever feel safe otherwise, for the rest of my life, being punished by fear from him. If he knew I was with you Tan, talking about him, we would both get beaten. We can't feel this anytime we are in the same place. I need him gone, for good. I know you can sort it Julie, please."

"Tania, I can't let..." pleads Julie.

Pauline holds out a wad of cash for temptation., and waves it like a fan. "To cushion the blow."

"Julie, we need this. This is spiritual stuff, we have been guided here. I asked the universe and look, here it is. It's called an affirmation of abundance right there."

"Babe, come on, seriously?"

"Trust me Juuulliieee. I can feel a presence, a gut feeling, I just know." Tania takes the money out of Pauline's hand and starts to put it in Julie's bra.

"Here, you need a bit of extra padding, you're too B cup. We can't carry that cash around." Tania looks deep into Julies eyes, she knows she has Julie in the palm of her hand with those sultry eyes. "We can do this, we're a team aren't we?"

Pauline's phone rings, it's Gary's name on the screen. Pauline starts to shake and looks like she's going to have a panic attack. Julie and Tania sit her down.

"Answer it." Julie comforts Pauline. "Don't let him know you have company."

"Hello." Pauline's voice has a slight quiver.

"Can you come over? We need to talk." Gary slurring his words and clearly off his face.

Pauline looks at Julie and Tania, who are huddled up trying to listen, and Julie nods 'yes'. "Talk about what?"

"About us. You're so great at role-play, just like today, looking all sexy sat there on the beach, wind in your hair, totally acting innocent and up for it."

Pauline's rage burns up inside, but tries to keep it cool, without knowing she's being too blunt. "Up for it? No one wants what you did, you...." Pauline pauses to see Julie mouthing the words "Be nice" to her. Pauline changes her tone instantly. "You...are so passionate aren't you? You were so horny today, all man, with your muscles and your power. I'll make my way over shortly if that's alright?" Pauline knows he's probably setting her up but plays it perfectly.

"Cool, I'll crack open some bubbly."

"Make it a nice one Gary. I feel like tonight should be a special toast, a real celebration."

"Grrr, you sexy little devil. Get that ass over here and I'll have a top-notch bottle on ice." Gary slurring his words even more.

"Sounds perfect. How about some more role-play? Leave the door on the latch and be in bed, naked. I'll sneak in and undress and crawl onto the bed on all fours and you do whatever you want to me, Sir."

"Phwwooarrr too bloody right. Gonna jump in the shower and make myself clean and fresh for ya, down there, if you know what I mean. See you soon honey suckle."

Pauline gags and cringes." Yeah, bye, see you soon babe."
Pauline turns to Julie and Tania.
"That level of denial is the biggest red flag ever to hit me in the face, he's mental. You know where he lives don't you Tania?"

"I sure do, lots of negative memories there. I'm seeing full circle in my third eye, so this means..."

"Yeah we get it Tan. Have you got some white sage to smother whilst we're there? Julie adds. Pauline and Tania laugh together. "Honestly Pauline she will say she has wings next."

"Actually, come to think of it."

"NOPE! That's enough." Julie stamps her foot down. "Come on

let's go. Polly, go and have a hot bath, rest up and let's lay all this carnage to rest."

"I owe you one."

"No you don't - after everything you did for me years ago, I'll never forget it." Tania looking affectionately at Pauline. "You'll always be part of my Akashic records up there..." pointing to the sky.

"Dear lord." Julie sighs.

"Come here you two." Pauline kisses them both on their cheeks. "Thank you, you're both angels."

"Don't you start as well." Says Julie, jokingly.

All three start to gently laugh, Pauline puts her hands together in the prayer position. "Namaste darlings."
Pauline walks off looking lighter, in a different direction, Julie and Tania hold hands and walk towards their car.

Julie instantly worried. "You do realise this could end up with us both inside for years?"

"We won't. This is his destiny. And we can pay off our rent arrears and put some towards your boob job."

"What boob job?"

"I mean, look, look at the proportion of you now your bra is stuffed with 20's, you need to expand the udders my lovely."

"You're lucky I love you or I'd knock you clean out."

"That's the spirit, keep that frame of mind. Dear Archangels, please keep myself and Julie safe and on the correct path. Surround us with love and light. Amen."

"Can't you just ask them lot to keep us out of jail and to get away with it or for them to just take him up there?"

"It doesn't work like that I'm afraid, it's how you say it. Spiritual manners are felt across the ether and many guides and angles can step in to help when they feel that powerful vibration coming from me. It's a gift."

"Where do you get all this random info from?"

"I'm connected to the source."

"Jesus Christ."

"Yes him."

Julie shakes her head and lights a joint. And points to it whilst looking at Tania. "Think him upstairs will mind?"

"No, not at all. Anything grown from the earth is his creation, so his fault really, he's fine with that though."

"You're one of a kind aren't ya."

"I sure am. Now let me inhale the magic."

Julie pecks Tania on the lips and passes her the spliff and gets into the drivers seat, Tania into passenger seat.
They drive off, in an old, loud, clunky mini.

Meanwhile, back in the Parlour, all girls are sat around the lounge dolled up, waiting for punters to ring or knock at door.
Pauline, looking washed out, puts on a front and tells the girls.
"I'm staying in my room tonight. I need a soak and pamper night. Andy will be on the door until morning."
Pauline looks at Andy affectionately, Andy and Pauline embrace.
"Thank you so much Andy. Who would you like your happy ending with?"

"Lush Lisa, please."

"I'm just a receptionist, I only..."

Pauline hot on her tails. "Aww thanks Lisa, you're such a good worker."

"But, Pauline..."

Pauline whispers into her ear; "After what I've been through lately"

"I'd love to suck you Andy, but I gag too much, I can't help it." Pleads Lisa.

Natalie jumps up from the sofa and shouts;
"I'll DO IT! I've literally got no gag reflex at all. Look at this."
Natalie grabs a banana out of the fruit bowl and pushes it all the

way down with a sultry look in her eyes, straight stare at Andy's eyes.

"WOW. Thanks all the same Lisa, but that's what I'm looking for. Where have you been my whole life?"

"Practicing."

"Knew I had you and that gob sussed when I met you. We need to think of a working name for you Nat."

"How about blow job Bella?" Leigh blurts out.

"Or Debbie deep throat." Lisa pleased she's got a name in too.

"Yes, that's perfect. Debbie deep throat it is." Pauline decides.

"Yes" says Sandra, with relief in her voice. "Finally someone who actually wants to suck. I can't bear it."

"Really? Could have fooled me. Thought you loved it. You've made loads from oral."

"I know Polly, but ever since that client pushed my head down too far after I'd just eaten fish and chips and I puked all over his tackle, I just hate it."

Andy is in fits of laughter and looking at the girls' conversation like he's at Wimbledon; left, right, back & forth, loving every minute of it.

"Polly, this is a bit of me innit. Beats working passion nightclub door 5 nights a week. I can do three here and two there, mix it up a bit if that suits?"

"Of course, it's fine Andy. I knew you'd like it in here. Just so you know everyone - Andy was a huge part of my life when I moved here; put me up, fed me when I was skint and has always been there for me. Andy, enjoy your shift, girls try and keep the fake groans at a lower level so I can sleep and keep her upstairs happy."

"She's moving away, so hopefully get a nice new neighbour." Sandra reveals.

"How do you know?" Pauline grining at the news.

"Bumped in to her earlier, she's off to Europe for a year, last minute thing apparently."

Pauline deep in thought.

"Hmm. I could do with an extra flat, about time Polly's Parlour expanded. I can just see it now: 'Polly's Parlour 2', let people know I am here to stay. I'll pop up and see what the deal is."

Pauline exits and goes up to Nicki's Door. Pauline knocks and rings the bell, sees her lights on - but no answer. Pauline goes back down to her place and runs a bath and slips into a big bubble bath, with a glass of wine, and relaxes whilst listening to classic FM on the small radio on the side of her marble sink.

Pauline has had some thinking time and feels she needs to go back to therapy. Years ago she had two different therapists but did not feel they did much, apart from sit there looking like a librarian and kept asking - "So, how do you feel?" all the time.

Around five years ago Pauline was feeling low and someone suggested counselling and she dived into it.

After the 10th time of her therapist asking that annoying question, Pauline snapped and replied, "How do you think I fucking feel. I have not come to therapy because I am happy have I? Does anyone come here full of the joys of spring?" With that she walked out and never went back.

But rumour has had it there's a tough talking counsellor working above a lampshade shop around the corner on the high street. She's heard he is on point, on the money and gets results.

Pauline makes an appointment for this morning and can't believe she got a slot straight away. Being new in Brighton, the counsellors clients are building slowly and he could hear something in Pauline's voice, which sounded like she needed it now, not tomorrow or next week.

There was a sense of urgency in her voice, which is why he slotted her in for 10am, when he doesn't usually start until lunchtime.

With this is mind she's feeling proactive, pleased with herself that she will try therapy again, which has put her in a great mood this morning.

Natalie is curled up asleep on the sofa. Lisa is asleep in one of the bedrooms, Sandra and Leigh have left. Pauline walks in and starts clearing a few cups and plates.
"Morning Natalie, time to wake up."

Natalie opens her eyes and immediately alert.

"Pauline, I'm so sorry, I had nowhere else to go and I didn't want to ask last night in front of everyone."

"It's ok, you can use one of the rooms until you get on your feet, plenty of room, but you'll have to pay your share in rent and bills."

"That's absolutely fine for me. I've been homeless before and picked myself up a few times. I was stupid to move in with my ex, I lost my council flat moving in with him."

"Been there myself Nat, you're welcome here, away from him. Come out the back for a cup of tea and a cigarette?"

Natalie attempts to get up but is in pain and winces and sits back down.

"Oh dear, I forgot, you tended to soldier Sean's needs. You rest and have a bath, you did well for a first shift. How was Andy's...you know?"

"It was...errrmm...bendy."

"Like a banana?"

Natalie smirks."No, umm, just an odd shape with a deep purple head. Never seen one like that."

"Trust me Nat, after half a lifetime of men I can assure you they come in many sizes and weird shapes. As long as he enjoyed it and he left emptied and happy."

"He most definitely loved it, it was over really quickly."

"A lot of them are. It's all mouth about being able to go all night and when it comes to it, they are weak and fragile. It's called 'tricks of the trade' and 'turning tricks' for a reason."

"What do you mean?"

"When your arm gets cramp, or your jaw hurts and they are taking their time to climax that's when we turn up the tricks. Softly whisper over their ears how amazing they are and how much you love their dicks, run your nails down their back, lick the neck, put your finger round the back if need be, then watch them climax. Save those intimate tricks for the ones who take too long."

"Doesn't it matter if they pay for an hour but finish early?"

"God no. Once they have sealed the deal they are worn out and most are married, so the guilt starts to kick in and they can't leave soon enough. Apart from the younger ones on their way home from clubs. Now they are fine with a five-minute break and can go again, randy little buggers."

"So, take the rough with the smooth?"

"You got it. You'll learn fast girl. Remind them of the tip jar, how you'd love to service them again and if someone doesn't ask the price on the phone, then add extra. Once they are here and raring to go, like a horse at the start of a race, they don't think business, they think of pussy, so the pounds don't get a look in. Maximum income for minor output, that's my motto."

"I'm so glad I met you. I know I can be a bit of a mouthy cow, but life has thrown too much at me for my age. I'm defensive because I try to protect myself."

"You're in your 20's, in your prime. Anyway I like girls with a bit of an edge and I get a good feeling about you. That's why I gave you my card. You're a keeper and whilst in the house of Polly, I'll do all that I can to help you. Go and have a bath I'll bring you in a cup of tea."

"I will do. Again, thank you."

Pauline rubs Natalie's arm as she walks off towards the kitchen.

09.45am approaches and Pauline has managed to get everything in order and ready for her therapy session, but has nerves and doubts. Opening up her secret inner world to a stranger, she knows is daunting and is not sure what she will talk about, or if there will be a connection between her and the counsellor.

Arriving at the door, Pauline almost walks away, but feels this is the right time, and is pleasantly surprised when the counsellor opens the door in a pink polo-shirt, jeans and loafer shoes.

"Welcome Pauline, I'm Terry. Please, take a seat."

Pauline has a quick glance around and likes the feeling; a colourful room, with candles & crystals and the big leather chair for her is inviting.

Pauline was expecting a long old stiff introduction about how things work and what's on offer, all done mechanically and not personal. However, Terry gets to the point.

"What goes on here is strictly between me and you. This is 'our' space, use it how you feel most comfortable. I want you to come here and feel it's a space where you can totally be yourself, with no judgements, no airy fairy chat, just laying your inner self out to look at, together. How does that sound?"

Instantly Pauline feels like she has sunk into the chair and is looking at someone genuine and totally in his element.

"That means a lot to me. Already this feels different. I had therapy before and they were useless, you seem a world away from them."

"I pride myself on being invested in my clients. I'm not here to just sit and listen, it's a joint effort, a process, an experience we share. See it as a journey of self discovery. I am here to make sure you are safe and protected whilst doing so."

"I feel so relaxed already - I could fall asleep."

Terry smiles at Pauline. His warm reaction makes her feel welcome.

"I don't know where to start really."

"How about sharing why you felt the need to come here today?"

"I've been through a lot in my life and I don't think I've ever dealt with it properly."

"Such as?"

Pauline freezes.

"Pauline, we do this at your pace. If at any point it feels too heavy, we can take a break and go back to it, no pressure needed in here."

"I'm confused and I am...fucking angry."

Pauline surprised this would come out of her own mouth.

"What makes you feel this way?"

"A lifetime of searching for love and never found it, not fully I don't think."

"What has that search been like for you?"

"Sexual exploration mostly, reaching out to my mum, selling myself, relationships. All areas left me empty, hollow, nothing."

"I can understand why you would feel that way, but you are not empty, you have love to give, that's why you're looking for somewhere to direct it. When we can't get it to our desired location, it remains inside and when internalised it can make you feel as though you are void of feeling, when it's the opposite. A heart which has love to give is not empty."

"I've never looked at it that way."

Terry continues.

"How did you try to explore that with mum and lovers?"

"I was submissive to them all. I fully let them in, only to be hurt over and over."

"So being submissive never worked?"

"Well, no."

"What happens in your life when you're not submissive?"

"Um, I guess, I'm not sure."

"Work, friendships? What are you like in those environments?"

"Oh totally in control, I don't take no shit." Terry stares at her and uses silence, the penny drops for Pauline.

"Ah, I see, yes - I get results from standing up for myself and taking the lead."

"In what way could you implement that in amongst your search for love?"

"I could just be me, not submit to please anyone."

"When you say 'be me" - who are you?"

"I'm Pauline, born Paul." Terry doesn't react, Pauline tries more, to see his reaction.

"I transitioned years ago and I own a brothel."

She uses the word brothel because she feels he will think it's a beauty salon if she says parlour and wants to hit him hard with her truths.

Still, Terry doesn't flinch. One last try to see if he budges or judges.

"My parents were cunty to me."

Terry may as well be frozen, she will not be getting the same reaction people have given in the past. This, she realises, is a closed space, a place where she has the freedom to express everything.

"So you're Pauline who owns a brothel."

"You missed out the trans part."

"Do you want to talk about that part?"

"Isn't it important?"

"I don't know. Is it important to you? What feelings are coming up for you whilst you ask that?"

Pauline looks out of the window, day dreaming, avoiding. Terry lets her think.

"I feel like it's hurt me a lot of times in my life, but by other people. My identity was overbearing when I was younger, it hurt my head. I knew I was different from my friends but I was so happy with who I was inside, that I could never understand why people did not like me or judged me. So twenty years ago I had my surgery and it changed my life, but sadly not those around me."

"What people?"

"My mum, men. They rejected me even more, I felt."

"So external noise and negativity from others. What were your feelings around that change?"

"I felt amazing because I took charge and made the decision to take the lead on my own life, where I would live, work and play."

"So, when not being submissive you get the results you want?"

Pauline realises she has played right into therapy and revealed herself.

"You're bloody good Terry. Yes, I succeed when I take the lead and don't give in to other people's ideas and judgements."

"So, you're not void of feelings, you have a lot to share with someone, and being who you are today, your authentic self, makes you happy?"

"Exactly that - I am stronger than I think."

Pauline processes this and remains quiet for a moment. Terry sips some water as Pauline starts to cry.

"It's ok to let it out Pauline, here have one of these." Terry passes her a box of tissues. "What's upsetting you?"

"When I think back at men who have beat me because they found out I was a biological man, before and after surgery. I don't tell anyone because no one ever guesses, and it's like breathing air for me; it's just a part of who I am, not the one thing which is the whole of me."

Pauline is starting to glow, more alert and seems happy to talk.

"I am proud of myself for that. I will always be honest if someone asks me, but I describe myself as human being, first and foremost. When someone comes out of the closet, say twenty years ago, do they need to add the 'I am gay' label to their self description in conversations? It's a moment in time, in the past, which is personal and something I like to keep to myself."

"When describing yourself to me, you referenced being trans."

"That was just for shock value. I don't actually introduce myself as trans."

"Because?"

"Because I can't take any more punches or negativity from people. It serves no purpose. So I have turned it into a positive, and that is to share it when I feel I want to."

"So you are taking the lead on whom you share your past with?"

"Yes, I am."

"How is that working out for you?"

"I have lived here for 10 years and barely anyone knows, because it doesn't matter. My way is very healthy for me."

"To recognise where and what makes you happy, to then implement something you can handle, all sounds like it's working for you."

"Protecting myself is paramount. I guess I am successful, when you look at it that way."

"Where is the anger?"

"Attached to my past. My parents, ex's and that bitch Belinda."

"Who's Belinda?"

"A friend, I mean, was a friend, now my enemy."

"I can see your body tense up as you mention her. Would you like to explore that?"

Pauline is tapping the side of the chair.

"I hate her. It's not even a her; it's a man in a fucking frock. Cock in a frock. VERMIN. Oh Terry, I'm so sorry."

"No need to apologise, honestly, this is the place to let all that out. What happened between you and Belinda?"

"I was seeing someone for a long time, post op. I had a crush on him for a long time and he asked me out to dinner, and from that moment we were stuck to each other for a year. I had only felt like that once before, when I was 18. He proposed to me, I said yes and I was smitten. Belinda came down from London to live with me and decided to 'accidentally' mention my transition surgery when talking about my tits. She knew he didn't know, I told her several times to be careful.

I had left London to start a new life and get away from the bad boys I had met, it was all amazing here for me. She ruined it in one minute flat. She was lucky I was not there or I would have killed her. He came to my door and said nothing - just kicked the hell out of me. I was on the floor whilst he was punching, slapping, kicking and stamping on me."

Pauline starts to break down and cries like she's never cried before, lifts her knees-up to her chin and sits to the side, staring at the floor.

Terry lets silence fall for a few minutes.

"Does Belinda know how you feel or what happened?"

"No way, uh uh, she is never gonna know either. Wouldn't give her the satisfaction knowing I got battered. I knocked her out in a bar one night, and recently punched her, that has made me feel better."

"Losing a friend, being betrayed and then beaten, is very sad. Your angry feelings are valid, totally. What would you like to do with that anger?"

"Let it go, park it somewhere, I don't know, I want rid."

"We can explore that in future sessions, I think it will benefit you greatly. You've carried this for a long time. It's YOU that has done that, you've got through it yourself, that's a tough ask of anyone. Talking about it here is highlighting areas I hope you are proud of."

"Thank you. Coming from a therapist that means a lot to me."

"All the other parts are exterior, outside influences, noise and opinions. How does it feel not to have that negative reaction in here?"

"It feels amazing to be totally authentic. I feel, strange, in a good way. I've been honest with friends, not many, but this is just about me, it feels.....beautiful, to be heard properly. This is how I want to feel more often."

"How might you get this outside of this room?"

"I don't know."

"Is there an area of your life where you would like to feel this?"

"Yes, in a relationship. But I'm single."

"Can you tell me what that relationship looks like in your head?"

"It's me being valued for being myself, a man looking at me for who I am inside. A relationship where I am heard, seen and loved for ALL of me, and doesn't want to let me go."

"How would you be able to tell if someone was all accepting and all loving towards you?"

"I would be able to tell if he loves loving me. I would feel it in my heart, I just know it. I feel there's a place inside for someone, without it taking over or being sad."

"Sounds like you know what you want?"

"A healthy relationship where I can be real."

"You already have the answers inside, you just need to tap into them. Therapy will help you connect with the tools you need."

After discussing her parents and her current situation, minus Gary details, Terry brings the session to a close when the hour is up. Pauline feels lighter, happier and a sense of freedom from the past. Feeling this after one session has given her hope she will succeed at therapy. Pauline makes an appointment for next week and leaves there like she's walking on air.

Sheila and Robert return from being all night together, bright and breezy. Robert holds Sheila and kisses her and thanks her for a lovely night.

"Have a good day at work babe."

"Don't call me that please. It's so generic."

"Really? Sorry, I thought you liked pet names."

"Yeah, like, a unique one, not one half the world uses."

"Bloody hell, you're coming out of your shell. Like what?"

"Think of one. Think about what you feel for me, see in me,

something more special."

"BUSTY?"

"Oh my God."

"I'm kidding. Even though they are a cracking pair. Well, I don't know. Ahh, I know, I know.....how about - my sunlight."

"Ahh that's sweet. Why that?"

"Because you bring light into my dark heart."

Sheila looks like she's blushing and cuddles Robert.

"Awww, have a nice relaxed day at mine, sorry it's a bit small and rough."

"It was cozy last night, we could get something bigger in no time if you wanted to. I'll call in later to speak with Pauline about some work."

"Her mobile number is next to the phone at mine, she's always busy, and in and out, so call her on that. See you later."

"Speak later sunrise."

"What the hell Robert?"

Roberts laughs. "Ok, sorry, sunbeam."

Sheila starts to laugh. "Sunbeam? What am I - a bloody canal boat? You're such an idiot sometimes. I have missed this you know, no one makes me laugh like you do."

"This could be a new life for us and last night was just the beginning."

Sheila puts her finger over his lips. "Ssshhh. We don't need to talk about last night. I don't want to know where you went."

"I meant in the bedroom, as if it was the first time again, only you added a few extra layers of passion. I didn't know you could do all that, you little minx."

Sheila looks really proud of herself and smiles.

"The sun is a bright star, hence why that came into your head about me. I'm glowing and I'm gunna blow up your world."

Sheila flicks her heel back and up and lifts her shoulder with a seductive look in her eyes, licks her finger and touches her upper body with it.

"Tssss. I'm piping hot, babe."

"Generic!"

"Yeah, Byyeeee."

Sheila blows him a kiss as she walks down the steps. Robert shakes his head in a loving way and walks off smiling.

Sheila bumps into Pauline when she enters. the Parlour.

"Morning Sheila, wanna coffee?"

"Ah, I'd love one."

"So would I, get the kettle on and make Natalie a tea. One for Lisa too, I'll wake her up then you can tell us all how it went last night. LISAAAAA - get up, tea here for ya."

"OK, I'm up already."

"Can you quickly make up that single bed in the office, it came yesterday. Bedding is on the desk. Might have that as a space for someone who's coming this week."

"I'll do that now." Phone rings and Lisa picks up. Hello Polly's Parlour. Oh my god Layla, how are you?"

Pauline's sudden realisation she forgot to see her last night.

"Oh shit ,shit, shit. Lisa, pass me that." Lisa passes her the phone.

"Layla I'm soooo sorry I was due to..."

"It's ok I'm not there anyway."

"What? Why not?"

"I signed myself out yesterday afternoon after I spoke to you Polly. There's nothing showing on my scans and it looks worse than it is. I've got loads of valium and painkillers to keep me happy. I am staying with my sister for a week or two, and heal. I just spoke with the police, they've not found out who did this to me and I can't for the life of me remember anything yet. The last thing I recall is popping out to my car to get something and a car pulled up. I remember a man asking for a quickie and I said yes as I had a gap in the diary and it was a quiet night. I can't see his face in my head though."

"You don't recall the cucumber?"

"A cucumber? No, Christ no. Copper said it may all come back to me."

"Let's hope so Layla. You recall the car?"

"Just dark, that's all I could tell the police. Who could do this to me? We've never had any trouble. I'm still shaking."

Pauline looks guilty and on the verge of saying who she thinks it is but feels such sympathy and guilt she stops herself. "Every dog has its day and whoever did it will feel the Karma, one day."

"Hope so. Right, my sister has my breakfast ready and I need to pop a pill or two and rest up my halloween head."

"Only you could crack a joke at a time like this."

"Not the first time in my life I've taken a battering, we crack on don't we Polly?"

"We sure do. Don't come back until you are fully rested and healed. I'll send you some cash to tide you over, for food and stuff."

"There's no need, my sister will take care of me."

"It's called sick pay doll. And I won't take no for an answer."

"Ok Momma Polly."

"Ring me whenever you want. Bye darling."

Pauline hangs up and sits on the reception chair and ponders on her thoughts. Pauline remembers Lisa sits on the chair.

"LISA - have you just sat on this chair?" She calls out.

"Yeah, why?"

"Vile. With no knickers on I bet?"

"No, actually, I've got these."

Lisa pulls up her skirt to reveal the same bright orange, fluffy, crotchless knickers the client gave her to put on, two days ago."

"For fuck sake, they're crotch-less. Wipe the seat down, now. I'm just popping up to see Nicki."

Lisa trying to laugh it off but very embarrassed as she nonchalantly reaches for the wet wipes and wipes seat.

"Best of both worlds; fashionable and I get the breeze I need. I hated them at first, I'm liking these middle ground knickers now."

Pauline shakes her head and leaves to walk up the steps to see if Nicki is in. Nicki opens the door.

"Well, good morning. To what do I owe the honour?"

"Pipe down Nicki, it's too early for sarcasm."

"You've never ever knocked my door."

"I didn't, I rang the bell."

"Now who's being sarcastic?"

"A little birdie tells me you're off travelling?"

"Yes, France first, leave tonight. My flat mate left the other day, can't afford this on my own, why?"

"Fully furnished you rented it for didn't you?"

"Yes. What's with the sudden interest in me?"

"I need the flat. Who's the landlord?"

"Can't say."

"What?"

"I'm doing a runner. Need every penny for my travels. It's a last minute decision, so I could do without you ruining for me."

"Great, so he's not going to welcome me with open arms if I say I know you. How much rent do you owe?"

"About a grand."

"Give me his number, when you've gone I'll ring him and say I've heard you've done a runner. I'll offer him cash up front."

"Aww, anyone would think you care Polly."

"Listen, Nicki, I had your back covered for a long time and let you stay on longer than you should have. I warned you numerous times to buck up, but you didn't. Now you're leaving I'll call a truce, and wish you well on your travels. Learn to move your hips a bit and grind a little, it'll work wonders when you meet someone."

"Are you actually giving me tips on how to perform in the bedroom?"

"See it as feedback from your previous employer. Besides, it's what the clients were saying too, so you have that little bit of free advice and find yourself a nice man to move those hips with."

"Really? A man? Pauline look at me; skinhead, tattoos, rainbow flag. Any bells ringing?"

Pauline looks at the flag, looks her. "How could I possibly miss that? I thought the hair was because of your catholic stuff?"

"Eh?"

"You know, trying to be like Sinéad O'Connor."

"Mary mother of God, what on earth."

"So that's why the lack of movement with the men? Why didn't you say?"

"I don't know. It just felt weird being gay and working for you. I thought you may not want me working there. I've always looked up to you and I didn't want to lose you as a mate or as a boss, and I ended up losing both roles with you. You know I'll forever have your back."

Pauline cracks a smile. "Good luck to you Nicki, I appreciate..."

Interrupting from walking up behind Pauline, is John, the client who Nicki saw the other day. "Good mooooorning Polly. Nice to see you again. I was just passing and wondered on the off chance of the same as the other day?"

Nicki's face is frozen and gobsmacked. Pauline is looking totally confused as to why he's calling her Polly.

"Sorry, I don't think we've met. I'm Polly."

"Two Polly's, what are the chances!"

"Nicki, care to explain?"

"He knocked my door, I needed money, so I saw him as a client."

"You did fucking what? Always have my back? You lying dirty dyke. I hope your plane crashes tonight."

"I'm going by ferry."

"Fuck you Nicki."

"Pauline please, let me explain."

"John, come with me. My Parlour is the apartment below. You, young lady, will always, always, be a let down to me."

"He's into scat, thought I'd be doing you all a favour by seeing him."

"I haven't got time for this shit, literally. Tell you what Nicki, have him, plenty of bullshit comes out of your mouth, double whammy John, off you trot."
Pauline pushes John back towards Nicki and goes back down to her Parlour. Nicki, furious but embarrassed, slams the door in John's face."

Pauline walks into the lounge, with just Lisa there, who is sat on the sofa in front of TV, watching the local news. An anchor man delivers the news;
"The police have discovered a body on the East Side of Brighton, in what police say was a 'horrific murder.' The family has been contacted and comforted by our team of specialists and would appreciate privacy at this sad time."

Pauline and Lisa look at each other, both with eyes widened and in silence. The news continues;
"The man, aged 35, has been named as Gary Woolmington. Police are asking anyone with any information, no matter how small, to please come forward and help them with their inquires".

Lisa looks frozen. Pauline falls back into her chair, in shock.

CHAPTER FOUR

Matthew

Pauline is having a major flash back to her childhood. She is sat in the front garden at home, on a rope swing hanging from a big oak tree, in a white dress, eating a lollipop. Drunken mother made it clear she never wanted a son, so he was dressed in girls clothes by her, yet still wasn't enough to make her a loving motherly figure in any way. Paul did not exist in her world, and his father had no connection with him either. Paul had to be a girl at home, and actually liked the frilly dresses and dolls. This created a little secret world at home where dress up became a fantasy world, lived out through his mother. Even if this hadn't happened, Paul would still have become Pauline; he was too feminine, too pretty and always felt detached from everyone and everything. Paul knew deep inside the body he was functioning in, wasn't the one that made him ever feel settled, just always a constant battle inside. There was a void, an unhappiness and a lost feeling. All the kids in the neighbourhood did not want to play with the 'freak in the dress', only his best mate, Grant. This reaction from his peers and parents, and being an only child, planted a seed of disassociation, a fantasy world expressed to teachers and social services if anyone asked why he was off school, or had bruises or seemed withdrawn.

Paul made up a narrative, which was plausible, telling everyone mummy & daddy gave affection, played games, had lots of friends round and home life was beautiful, any bruises were from the rough and tumble of playing football in the garden with his father.

Father was just as distant and was a tall, chubby, dapper, trilby wearing aggressive figure.

On this day he pulls up with screeching tyres, storms through the gate and asks where mother is. Paul's body language is closed and inward, a clear indication he's scared. Paul points to the upstairs of the house and, with a tremble in the voice, gently tells him,

"In the bedroom daddy."

He runs upstairs and kicks open the locked bedroom door to see her with two other men in bed, naked.

A loud and aggressive argument sees Paul put his hands over his ears and waits until it's finished.

Father, with suitcase in one hand and a bag in the other, walks out of the house and down the path, passes Paul, and doesn't even acknowledge him. As he spins off, Paul runs to his bedroom and hides behind the door.

Mother, a glamorous lady with beehive hair, lots of makeup, wearing a pink silk & lace short night gown, leaves her bedroom with the two men, laughing, and all go downstairs. Paul creeps out of the room and looks over the stairs bannister to see both men hand his mother lots of money. Paul is noticed by one of the men, who assumes it's a girl, and calls up;

"Hey pretty girl."

Which stirs up fury in his mother's eyes.

When the men leave she charges at Paul, as if in a slow motion, flying for him, mouth frothing at the sides, screaming like a woman with the devil inside her. Paul puts his hands over his ears and shrivels up into the corner as she lunges forward and punches him in the head, several times.

"Pauline. PAULINE. MRS COCHRAN?" Police officer calls. out.

Suddenly Pauline slips out of her flashback and is tearful and has her hands over her ears, realising she has zoned out from the interview.

"Um, sorry, it's all this endless talk of how Gary was taken from me - I can't bear to hear it. He was a beautiful soul to me, a true gentleman."

"Pauline, we are able to let you go home now. Thank you for your co-operation, you've been a real help today, you're free to go."

"Are you any closer to finding out who did this to him?"

"I'm afraid we haven't just yet, but have a couple leads we shall be following, but this isn't the end - we WILL find the culprit, I'm sure. We've no further questions, unless there's anything else you would like to add before this interview comes to a close?"

"No, just, thank you for your help I just can't believe he's gone, bless him." Pauline's eyes well up and the police conclude the interview.

Pauline leaves the station, gets into her car, wipes away her face of running mascara. Pauline did cry, but it wasn't for Gary, it was for the memory lane she'd just been down. The police asked Pauline to go in as her 'Polly's Parlour' card was by Gary's bed.

Pauline spoke with them and did not feel she was a suspect, more sad girlfriend who's just lost what could have been the love of her life. Relief is present on her face, as is worry in equal measure. Pauline turns on her mobile and hears a voice mail from Maddie.

"Hi it's me, again, Maddie D, in the wheelchair, just ringing to see if I can drop by today, actually my Dad would drop me, anyway, please text to let me know if this is OK. Cheers Pauline." Pauline sighs, texts her 'YES', then drives off back to Polly's Parlour.

Pauline walks through her door, looking drained and flat, and bursts out laughing as she sees Sandra and Leigh dressed in Nun's outfits; skirts way too short, fishnets, 6" inch bright red stilettos and rosary beads in hands.

"What the fuuuuuuuu?" Pauline is tickled by this and can't get her words out.

Leigh announces like she's delivering a serious sermon; "Bless you Mother Polly, may the Lord be with thee today."

Pauline continues to laugh and struggles to talk. "Jesus, if you're watching, please forgive us! Girls, honestly, the least two people to be virgins. I can't cope looking at you."

Sandra and Leigh are lapping it up; twirling, laughing, licking the beads, lifting their habits up to reveal see through lace underwear and sliding up & down the wall. Lisa and Natalie have come to the hallway to join in and everyone laughing. The electric energy in Polly's, is always contagious and puts a smile on the girls faces daily. Pauline speaks through tears of happiness.

"You lot make my day you know. This is my home, this is my little family, this is where I belong."

"Here, here." Lisa agrees and gives Pauline a peck on the cheek. "Aww. How was it?"

"Draining, sad, long and actually life affirming. With death comes new beginnings, right girls?"

"Sure does. They found the killer?" Leigh asks.

"No, but they will do their best, I'm sure." Pauline winks at Lisa. Someone half knocks the front door and on the camera it looks like a man with his hands full, so Pauline opens the door.

"DELIVERY!" he says very cheerfully.

Standing there is a man holding Maddie in his arms, and her folded up wheelchair next to him."

"Oh my... it can't be. Matthew?"

"Polly? Holy shit. I've not seen you for years, wow, you look amazing. How are you babe?"

Maddie's father Matthew is 42 years old, salt and pepper short hair, green eyes, handsome, dressed in light blue denim jeans, Nike trainers and an OASIS T-shirt.

"God, it must be over 20 years now, what a lovely surprise."

"Polly, I was only thinking of you the..."

"Uhhhh Hellloooo. I'm still here, in mid-air." Maddie barks.

"Sorry, just, it's bloody Polly Cochran."

"I know, but you know I don't like heights. Chair please."

Matthew lowers her into the chair as he's trying to open it with his knees. Pauline steps forward to help him and their hands touch. Matthew looks at Pauline deep in the eyes and it's apparent there's chemistry there. Matthew hasn't even noticed the nuns because he has been so fixated on Pauline.
"Lovely to see you again Maddie. Come on through"

Matthew a bit shell shocked.
"Thanks, we....Oh, nuns, hello."

Pauline, through nerves, lets her vocal range squeak high;
"This is Matthew and Maddie everyone."
With a hot flush, showing in her red face.

Matthew greets them all with a kiss on the cheek and does the cross sign over himself when he gets to Sandra and Leigh.

"Bless me Father, for I have sinned." Leigh flirts.

"On multiple occasions I should imagine."

"Dad, don't be rude."

Pauline defends him. "Don't you worry Maddie, we love humour in here, keeps the spirit alive. Please, come on through to the office."
As they enter the office Maddie notices a small single bed in the corner, made up with frilled cushions, a tartan throw and fairy lights on the head board.

Thrilled at the sight of it she gets excited. "Would that be my work station?"

"Yes, you like it?"

"It's quirky, small, but yeah, I could make it work."

"Thanks for the voicemail, I can tell you're keen as that's the third one you've sent."

"I know what I want and the minute I saw that neon light out there I felt so drawn to it, like, this is where I'm supposed to be - "POLLY'S PARLOUR." Trust me, I'm good at my job. I've got good work ethics and I can work long hours."

"She got that from me." Matthew proudly says whilst a lingering look into Pauline's eyes.

"Which bit?" Pauline asks flirtatiously.

"All of it; professional, hardworking and reliable."

"Actually I'll give you that Matthew. There was never any issue with you, it was with your mates, they were a bad influence on you."

"I know, but that was a long time ago. I still can't believe it's you, after all this time. Back then I got lost on the party scene and moved to the country to settle and moved here with this young lady about two months ago. We had a horrific car..."

"Yeah, I've already told her about how you killed Mum."

"Maddie, don't talk like that in front of Polly please".

"I meant by accident. Besides, Polly doesn't want to hear doom and gloom do you Polly?"

Pauline a tiny bit irked she is addressing her as Polly already, but hides it well. "Perhaps me and your father can have a catch up in private one day, if you'd like that Matthew?"

"I'd very much like that, yes, yes I would."

Again Pauline and Matthew lock eyes and Maddie notices.

"Oh my days, really? Dad this could be my new boss. So Polly, what chances do I have as making it as a Pollette?"

"That's funny, a Pollette! I may use that from now on. Well usually people can call me Polly when I have known them a while and have my trust, apart from punters of course. But, seeing as me and your father go way back, then you can be a Pollette. So, logistically, what about getting to the bathroom etc without your dad to help?"

"I've got a commode at home I can bring in, so fewer trips to the bathroom. And I can keep wipes by the bed."

"Can you believe this is my daughter?"

"I can. I can see that glint in the eye with her too, you're alike. There's a lovely vibe between you both."

Matthew takes Maddie's hand. "I love you. I wish I could afford it so that you didn't have to do this. It's hard to hear you talk like this."

"It's just a job dad. There're big bucks in cripples."

Pauline cracks up laughing. "You're going to fit in just perfectly, the job is yours. I'll go through the rota and money later."

"I know how it all works, worked in one brothel before. It's a 70/30 split in my favour right?"

"Firstly, it's a Parlour. Secondly no, it's not, it's 50/50 split, which over time, if you prove your worth and hard work, will slowly rise towards a 60/40 - in your favour. Oh and there's a tip jar, we all make a lot on that and it's an equal share."

"Thank you. This will help us so much." Matthew says with a sense of relief in his voice.

"Yeah? I hear you're spending money on working girls occasionally."

Matthew looks at Maddie and shakes his head. "I have done yes. I had a good deal going at one whore house, sorry, I mean Parlour, near London, so haven't since we moved here."

"Liar dad."

"I don't care anyway Matthew, we all have desires, we all need a good time."

"I feel like I've done it all, had that experience and now I'm looking for something a bit deeper."

"When can I start?" Maddie interrupts.

"Now if you want? Let's go and speak to my girls and get you settled in. There's a website I am going to advertise on and put pics up, blur the faces, get me more punters through the door."

"Can't wait, Polly, thank you. I love money. I need to buy a jet engine to attach to this chair so I can get places quicker."

Pauline and Matthew laugh and nudge each other.

"Maddie, go on through to the lounge and I'll see your father out."

Maddie wheels herself out with a chirpy whistle and brazenly goes into lounge to meet the girls.

Pauline and Matthew are saying goodbye on the steps outside. Gazing into each other's eyes.

"So bloody lovely to see you Polls. You haven't changed a bit."

"Give over. Not heard anyone say Polls since you. You always were the charmer."

"You can trust me."

Suddenly Pauline's eyes become cold. That trust word just does not sit well with her and men, she stands back and half smiles, and shuts down.

"Anyway, thanks for dropping her in, I mean, escorting her in, oh bloody hell - anything I say feels wrong."

"Top tip from me - pretend the chair doesn't exist and treat her the same as everyone else. She's a feisty one and sees the chair as a hindrance."

"How long ago was the....sorry, how long has she been in the wheelchair?"

"Five years. And don't worry, nothing you can say would offend me, or her. I'm still the same, just older."

"I need to get back inside, I have a lot to catch up on with the girls."

Behind Matthew a man from the church appears; dog collar, glasses, grey hair and holding a bible.

"Hello father, please, careful down the steps."

Pauline links his arm as Matthew stands back, slightly shocked.

"Speak soon Matthew."

Pauline half smiles and walks back into the Parlour, leaving Matthew standing there with a puzzled look on his face.

Pauline calls Leigh and Sandra to the entrance of a bedroom door.

"Sister Mary Joseph and Sister Catherine, Father...." Pauline looks at the him.

"It's Father Humphries." He joyfully says.

"Ah, lovely. Father Humphries requests your assistance in the chapel, if you could follow us please."

Pauline leads him into the bedroom, with church candles lit, curtains drawn, church choir music playing softly on the hi-fi deck and guides him into a chair.

"God bless you Polly." Father kisses her on the hand.

Pauline bows her head. "And God bless you Father Numphries".

"It's HUMPhries." Father clearing up her mispronunciation, as politely as possible.

"Of course it is. Enjoy the seaman ladies."

"I think you'll find its Sermon."

Father slightly irritated that she's lowered the tone.

Pauline licks her lips at him.

"Of course I know that Father. I'm just a naughty girl, a prolific sinner."

Father opens his bible and starts reading quietly.

To the girls she instructs; "Well, you two do the lord proud and spread the.....word." Pauline puts her hands together in prayer and wishes them luck. Sandra and Leigh trying hard not to react with laughter.

In the lounge there's a lively vibe and Pauline looks pleased. "Right, Maddie, you seem to have been acquainted with the girls."

"Princess paraplegic we are going to call her." Natalie boasts.

Maddie spits out her drink and cries with laughter. "I love it!

That's why I'm Maddie D. If I was in the spice girls that would be my name."

"What does the D stand for?" Lisa asks.

"Disabled. I'd be disabled spice."

"Bloody hell. Well, we can't use that on the cards for the phone boxes, or on the website."

"Why not? It's big business," Leigh says. "I was actually gonna rob a chair once from the hospital and pretend to be paralysed, as I'd heard of a local lady who did it and she managed to buy a new car in a few months."

Pauline genuinely shocked. "Wow! Ten out of ten for creativity and forward thinking but, you Maddie, have a niche market. Let's make sure we get the men here for you and advertise it in a more sophisticated manner."

"They will be flocking around here once word gets out there's a new princess in town, on wheels." Maddie is buzzing.

"I've had plenty of calls at reception asking if there was anyone less able-bodied, or if I knew of anyone, anywhere."

"YES Lisa, book them in! I am soooo gonna make it, be rich and have my own bungalow, wide hallways and doorways to die for. Pure independence."

In the background we hear an almighty noise of father, yelling AMEN, AMEN and his groan, which turns to tears and him saying sorry a few times. Pauline bites her lip and looks at the girls, all sniggering.

"Ssshh. Let's get to work, come on. Where's Sheila?" Pauline asks Lisa.

"She's doing the late shift and Natalie is doing double shift and Leigh said she would work until late."

"Perfect. I've got a photographer coming in today to get us on my website."

Natalie looks uncomfortable. "I'm not sure about being online as I've never done this work before and if my parents find out I'm dead."

"Where are your parents?" Pauline asks.

"Not sure, they won't tell me where they live now."

"So what's the problem?"

"I am in the process of patching things up, via phone calls, but only because I need to get in their wills. I can't let them die and get nothing for having to put up with them my whole childhood."

"Why? What happened?"

"Rules and regulations, that's what."

"Isn't that just called parenting?"

"Normally yes, but they are stuck up, strict and never ever supported my decision to leave school, live with a sugar daddy and smoke pot. I mean, what's the harm in that?"

"Ah, I see. So kinda turned tricks before then Nat?"

"Sort of, only I fell for him. I do think it was his money that made him more attractive though. Money is so pretty when it's spread out like a fan and I wave it back forth to cool me down."

Pauline, Lisa and Maddie crack up laughing.

Through tears Maddie looks at Natalie. "You're so funny Natalie. I think I'm going to love it here."

"I am quite funny, I've always been told that, like, I should be on some kind of stage."

"Like stage for 4 cancer?" Maddie jokes. No one laughs and all look at Maddie surprised.

"WHAT? Why are you all looking at me like that?"

"Maddie, that's really harsh." Lisa makes clear.

"My dad killed my mum in a car crash so...."

"That doesn't mean you can throw the cancer card at me." Natalie displaying that she is a little upset.

"Are those your cigarettes?" Maddie says, as she points to 20 Benson & Hedges on the side.

"Yeah, why?"

"Just, you know, they..."

"Oh my god, you're actually hilarious Princess."

"Thanks. We should both be on stage. The chemo sisters."

"Oh my god." Lisa in stitches at her dark humour.

"Right come on you thespians, let's talk through the order of the day." Pauline interrupts as she takes out her Filofax and gets the Parlour diary off of Lisa and gets her business head on.

"Ok, so I've got Lisa here all day again until close, tick. Natalie you have oral with cowboy John next for one hour, tick. Then two hours with a newbie, not sure what he wants, then photo shoot, tick. Maddie next client to ring will be yours if he's ok with the, umm, the..."

"Go on, you can say it you know. I am aware I can't move the lower trunk."

"Sorry Maddie, just don't want to offend, after what you've been through."

"Seriously Polly, just say unique, because that's what I am."

Lisa smiles at Maddie. "Aww, you're so sweet. What would you like me to describe you as on the phone and cards?"

"34 DD, spicy, BJ specialist, lower body has zero pain threshold, bubbly working girl. And you can say I am disabled. Disabled dollars are gonna roll in."

"I like that, I'll write it down." Lisa exits, Sandra and Leigh walk in after letting father Humphries out.

Pauline calls out. "Girls, you have another double booking in half an hour for Nelly necrophilia."

Maddie's eyes light up. "What's that all about?"

Sandra crouches down to Maddie. "Oh you have to play dead, it's quite easy, I have a snooze. Never done a double with him before though."

"I'd be good at that."

"Yes, of course, how about you do him with me? Your first client here at Polly's Parlour? Would you like to do that with me Maddie?"

"YES PLEASE. I am sooo excited. Nudge me if I snore Sandra."

Sandra takes her nun's outfit off. "Let's go Maddie, in bedroom one. Realistic stones are ready."

"Stones?"

"Tombstones. We lay with it at our heads, like we are in a grave. He will bring a little spade and pretend to dig us up, then he will do his thing."

"Wow, that's mad. What's on the tombstones?"

"He writes different names on them whilst I am "dead". Last time when he left I looked at mine and it said RIP Sis."

"This is fab, I wanna see what he puts for me. What does he do then?"

"So, this is where it's a little bit creepy, but he pays extra. He will lick every part of your body and whisper how much he loves to smell your dead flesh and how your toxic heart lives on inside of him, then rigor mortis rimming is his finale."

"Finale?"

"When he's rimming he starts to say how much he appreciates the worms and bugs eating you and that they taste like little pieces of you - like snacks of death."

"How the fuck do people get their fantasies? So strange isn't it? I once had a guy jumping on the bed so hard I was flying up and down and couldn't hold on and he did it until I stumbled off the bed, then I had to pretend he'd paralysed the rest of me so had to lay still and show fear in my eyes whilst he had sex with me."

Pauline looking amused. "It still amazes me on a daily basis. We are lucky women to be able to take on these incredible fantasies. You must always remember that we are keeping some of these off of the street, from harming women. It's a safe space for them to explore, without harm or judgement."

"Tell that to Layla." Snaps Sandra.

"Pauline bites."Oiiii, that's enough of that. Watch your mouth."

"Who's Layla?"

"Maddie, I'll fill you in after Nelly has dug you up. Run along. I mean...wheel off." Maddie pushes her wheels forward with a huge grin on her face and Sandra leaves with her. Leaving Leigh, Lisa and Natalie sitting down.

"How you feeling Polly?"

"Lisa, I'm still in shock to be honest, my feelings are all over the place."

"Is there anything we can do? You need any time off?"

"Cheers but I'd rather keep my mind busy for now, I've got a few things to go out for in a minute."

"Just over a month he was in your life, nearly every day, so it must be strange. We will come to support you when it's the funeral."

"I don't close my business for a funeral, life goes on. I will pay my respects on the day and I will take you with me Lisa, someone to link on to, if you're alright with that?"

"Most definitely. I've been there with you sharing your stories of how good he was to you, so I'd like to be there with you. Will be nice to say goodbye with you." Lisa purposely letting it be known that he was only good to her in front of the girls, just in case.

Phone rings, Pauline answers, it's Sheila. "Can we meet Polly? Suzie's coffee shop on the corner?"

"Yes, I'll walk up now, see you in 5." Pauline calls out to the girls."Right you lot, get yourselves in the zone, I shall be back shortly. Enjoy." Pauline leaves the Parlour and power walks up the road.

Pauline meets Sheila in a small artisan cafe, with dried flowers hanging, small white tables with candles in the middle, bohemian cushions and run by hippie Sue, with purple hair and dripping in beads, bangles and purple DM boots. Sue takes coffees to them at the corner table as *Leftfield's* album, *Leftism*, is playing at quite a high volume.

"Fancy some spotted dick with your coffee?" Pauline offers Sheila.

"I can't eat, I feel sick."

"Oh God, not morning sickness?"

"No just, for you, because of what's happened?"

Pauline becomes flippant. "Nothing has happened, I don't know what you're talking about."

Sheila looks around to make sure no one can hear, then at Pauline. "I mean about Gary."

"We don't need to talk about it, it's alright, all done and dusted."

"They've questioned me and Robert too, obviously, but we aren't on their radar at the moment. I think I may go back up north for a bit though."

"What for? "That makes it look more suspicious."

"Polly, that night, Robert went off for a while on his own."

"And?"

"Think about it."

"Don't worry yourself, he doesn't even know where he lives."

"He followed him, he passed us and I pointed him out, Robert just left without hesitation."

"Sheila, he's gone, you nor I have blood on our hands, so forget about it. If the Police are happy with your timeline of events and no more questions, you'll be ok. Put it to the back of your mind."

"I'm trying."

"Has he said he did it?"

"Well, no, but..."

"I have everything in hand, relax Sheila, everything is going to be fine. I am not letting you go, you belong here."

"Sorry, it's just I'm anxious and not thinking straight."

"Be in at 7pm ok? We can have a little drink. Tell Robert he can cover in a couple of days as Andy is working at the nightclub. Tell him I'm sorry I've not replied, it's been kind of hectic. But let him know I can give him 2 nights a week to start with, as a trial, next week."

"Ah, that makes things better. It's doing my head in already, being in that bedsit with a single bed."

"You'll get a place, in fact, may be good timing. I'm after Nicki's old apartment, it's exactly the same layout out as mine. Let me see if I get it first, if not I will help you find something."

"You're amazing. You always sort my issues out and make me feel so much better."

"I'm Momma Polly - it's my job. All the more reason to stay down here."

"I miss my family sometimes, even though my parents are weird and religious, I do miss them."

"Take a weekend off soon and go see them, or get a hotel near them so you don't have to be with them all day. Might make you feel better. You've been here six months and look how well you're doing. I'm proud of you." This compliment makes Sheila shed a tear, Pauline wipes it with a serviette.

"No one has ever said that to me, apart from my mate at school when I put a cigarette out on a lads face for bullying her."

"I can't imagine you doing something like that, you're so quiet and humble. I love that about you. Silent assassin."

"I quit smoking after that as I got expelled. That was also the start of my downfall with my parents. They were all about love and forgiveness, reciting the bible, yet they couldn't forgive me, for anything I did, so I rebelled even more and slept with my dad's best mate. They've never forgiven me for that."

"My, my, aren't you the little dark horse. Maybe a good idea to not stay with them then. What would they do if they found out your job is an escort, lady of the night, a working girl?"

"No matter what word I used they would call me a prostitute and would disown me."

"They sound like a barrel of laughs, maybe I should come with you. Both wearing thigh high leather boots and mini skirts."

Sheila smiles wide, puts her hand over Pauline's and squeezes it, lovingly. "I would love to see their faces, maybe you should." Pauline and Sheila enjoy their drinks and enjoy people watching for a while.

Pauline walks slowly back down to the Parlour. It's sunny, lots of people saying hello, she feels good. When approaching her building she sees a man coming out of Nicki's old apartment. "Excuse me Mr. Are you the landlord of 48b?"

Landlord, Roy, is 65, short, slim, rosy red cheeks, drives an old gold Jaguar, beige suit and very friendly - shakes her hand. "I am indeed. I'm Roy, how can I help?" Roy looks her up and down very quickly and looks smitten at first sight.

"Hi, I'm Pauline. Someone told me who ever lived here has gone travelling and I am looking for somewhere to rent, immediately, can pay cash up front for 6 months."

"Well, that would save me so much time, are you local?"

Pauline plays on a grief angle. "Yes, sort of. I've just lost my boyfriend, he passed recently so I am very desperate and have nowhere. I am staying with a friend, Sheila, but it's small, we need a place to share." Pauline's acting is extremely convincing as she wipes a little tear she has managed to push out.

"You poor dear lady, so sorry for your loss. Would you like to come in and take a look?"

"Thank you so much, that would be lovely." Pauline links to his arm and Roy beams at this and doesn't question it, he just leads her into the apartment and shows her around this hippie pad. It has plenty of colour, and the exact lay out as Polly's Parlour, minus an extra small room/office space.

"I love this lay out, it's unique. I love the high ceilings. I'll take it, please Roy."

"Ok. I have to be honest with you; there is a brothel downstairs and sometimes it's a bit loud my last tenant said. She said the owner was lovely but the comings and goings can be a bit, you know, annoying."

"That's alright with me. Each to their own, I listen to a lot of music, so probably won't bother me."

"Then it's yours." Roy, still looking her up and down. "I will sort contract with you and your friend later in the week. Needs a good clean in here though."

"Leave that to me, will give me something to do. Thank you so much Roy, you're an absolute gentleman, not many left like you in this world unfortunately."

Roy looks like a cross between someone being turned on and having a heart attack at the same time. "My absolute pleasure. Here take my card and call me in a couple of days." His face getting more red as he looks at her.

"Bless you Roy." Gives him a peck on the cheek, which Roy loves.

Pauline takes out her cheque book and writes him a six months rent cheque and both exit the flat, both satisfied with this transaction. Roy gets in his car and Pauline gets her phone out and pretends to call someone as she waits for Roy to leave, then goes into her Parlour.

Back inside Pauline is thrilled to announce; "Guess what girls, we've got a new gaff, right above, so I need to get more staff. Lisa and Natalie can you put some cards up around the phone boxes please?" Plenty printed off in office."

Pauline gets a text. "And the photographer will be here in an hour he's said, he can set up with his stuff in my bedroom. Off ya go girls, do a quick round then be back to glam up. Haven't those girls finished in the grave yet?"

Lisa, "I put my ear to the door and heard him talking to the dead."

"Lisa, back on reception please."

"Yes Boss."

A short while later Pauline opens the door to Ken, the Photographer. Ken is 35, black bushy hair, quirky, coloured tank top, chinos, trainers and very tall.

"Ken, please do come in. Lovely to meet you. We are going to use this room, follow me."

Pauline leads him into her own personal bedroom. "Here, you can use this big room of mine and move about whatever you want."

"Cheers, cool, this is a great size."

"I want the pictures to look classy, no dildos or anything smutty in the shot."

"You're the client, what you say goes."

"Let me know when you've set up and we will sort out who's in line."

"Nice one, thanks. Any chance of a cuppa?"

"Sure, kitchen is just through there, help yourself." Pauline walks off to see Maddie and Sandra back in the lounge. "Oh they're back from the dead. Welcome back girls, how was it?"

"Very relaxing actually" Maddie seems satisfied she has done her first client at Polly's Parlour. "He was really gentle. When he left I looked at my headstone. He wrote RIP Trixie."

"Oh, that was his dog. Mine was RIP Mummy." Sandra laughs.

"Wow so he thought I was a dog, cheeky fucker."

"Fascinating stuff. Get yourselves cleaned up, the photographer is here. Leigh will go first, then Maddie, Sandra, Natalie and lastly Sheila."

Pauline takes a bag out into the rubbish bin when a brand new Land Rover pulls up next to her. A man gets out and introduces himself.

Lee, 30's, tracksuit, gold chain, sunglasses, baseball cap and stocky. "Polly?"

"Depends on who's asking."

Lee is smiling and seems kind. "I can see why people want to come here. I imagine it would be to see you mostly."

"I doubt it, it's more so for the girls, I run the place."

"Yeah, I've heard. You like to give yourself up now and then though don't you?"

Pauline edgy about his tone and stands back from him. "Only for the special ones, so on a rare occasion."

"If the price is right eh?"

"Listen sunshine, what do you want?"

"I want to know what happened to my brother, that's what I want lady." Looks her up and down. "If you are one that is."

"Sorry, you've lost me. Brother?"

"Yeah, GARY. Not forgotten him already have you?"

Pauline is trying hard not to show her worry but her pupils expand and her neck goes red. Pauline starts to play with her necklace, trying to hide her nerves with a stand-offish attitude.

"Of course not, how could I? We were a new relationship and I fell for him. I'm devastated and only know what the police have told me."

"Something doesn't add up and his big black bag is missing."

"I've no clue what you're talking about. What bag?"

"Nah, of course you don't. I'll be keeping my eyes and ears open, trust me on that. I won't rest until the killer is brought to my lap, so I can do what Gary would have wanted me to do."

"Which is?"

"To torture them."

Pauline has her head up and acts tough. "Gary would not have treated me like this, you're barking up the wrong tree. I would love to know what's happened so keep me in the loop, I was his lover not his enemy."

Lee steps forward and into Polly's Face. "That smells

like....bullshit. I knew my brother inside out and he never treated women nicely. He's gone, along with a bag of two kilos of coke and I won't stop until I find it - and his killer. See ya soon, PROZY."

Pauline stands frozen as Lee gets in his car, pulls away and makes the gun silhouette with his fingers. Pauline mutters to herself "Fuck." With heart pounding, sits down on the steps to calm herself down.

CHAPTER FIVE

Therapy

Shortly after, Pauline is stood in the doorway of her bedroom, watching Ken in his element and thriving when directing Leigh, in her little red riding hood outfit.

"Ok, Leigh if you could bend over slightly and look over your left shoulder at the camera - right in the lens, that's it, give it to me." Leigh feeling like a celebrity and gives attitude and class. Ken is clearly turned on; glasses steaming up and a nervous giggle. Pauline proudly watching.

"Work that camera darling, you look sensational."

Pauline walks towards the reception, see's Tania on the camera and lets her in, even before she rings buzzer.

"Tan, should you really be here? At least right now?"

"Yes Polly, it's cosmic mate, really important." Both quickly walk into the office, Tania throws envelope at Pauline, onto the desk.

"What's this?"

"Your money. We didn't feel it was right."

"Don't be silly, you need this and you deserve it."

"We didn't do it Polly, we couldn't go through with it. We both smoked too much weed and had a whitey in the car, so pulled over and ate chocolate then fell asleep."

"Shit!"

"What?"

"You've seen the news right?"

"No, why?"

"Tan, he's fucking dead."

"Whaaatt? But, what? How, when?" Tania spinning out on the news.

"I really thought it was you. I've tried to ring you a few times."

"Ran out of credit and been monged out on this new skunk weed that's about. Fuck, I'm paranoid now. Hang on, let me ask my guides."

"Tan, this isn't the time for that, I need to think, fast. If you didn't, then? My heads in a spin."

"I'm hearing in my head that it's fate and it was taken out of our hands Polly. I asked my guides for protection that night and this is it. You and me are free of him, free of prison. My heart chakra is buzzing right now. This is a blessing." Pauline deep in thought and zones out.

"Thought you'd be pleased he's gone?"

"Shh, keep it down will you. I am pleased, it's all just sinking in you know - what we've been through, how its panned out, death, worry, joy, and now just..."

"Spit it out."

"It's Lee."

"Nooo. His one and only ally in this world has always been him. I get that being orphans keeps that bond but Lee was always so controlling over Gary, a bit too overprotective. Borderline schizophrenic someone once called him."

"He's been here, outside, threatening me."

"But you've not done anything wrong."

"Haven't I? I still wanted it to happen, for money. He knows Gary would not have treated me great, like I tried to convince him he did. Although he really did, I mean really lovely - until he found out about this place. Maybe his brother never saw that nice side."

"Gary was toxic, end of. Whether he found out about this place or not, it would only have been a matter of time, look at what he did to me. He needed taking out from this life, he was never going to be walking amongst angels on this earth plane, he belongs in the flames of dark realms. Do not pity that darkness. I hate to be the spirit of bad news but, his brother is the same, if not worse."

"Great, that's all I need in my life, another psych ward escapee. I need to get Lee off my back. I don't want to breathe the same air as him."

"Stick to your story; you liked him, it was only a 4 week "relationship" so it was new and fresh, he was kind to you, and you're gutted he has died. That's all that needs to leave your lips."

"Yes, I know you're right, but still, I need to just crack on and try to forget him. Thank you, Tan, for everything. Here, have this." Pauline hands her some of the cash.

"500 there for ya. The intention was there and I know you're skint, so pay your bloody rent and have a night out."

"Ya see, I prayed this morning for a new abundance and here it is. Thank you angels. Thanks Polly, you're a star."

"My pleasure. I ...." Phones rings, and she sees its Matthew. "I better go, we have a busy day. I'll see you soon darling."

"Any time. Love and light my lovely."

Tania exits, Pauline answers home phone, "Hello, how may I help?"

"Ello Treacle tits."

Pauline blushes and eyes light up. "Sorry, who's this?"

"You know exactly who this is. Who else would call you that?"

"Surprised you remembered it was so long ago, and you were off your head then."

"I will never forget that night, my sweet."

Pauline is laughing and has a reminiscing look in her eyes. "It was special, in that barn, all night. God, we were so young and care free then. I miss that feeling."

"So let's recapture some of it and find some fun, away from all this grown up shit. Life is so heavy and kills my back carrying around all this trauma."

"That's so funny."

"What is?"

"You - carrying around this humour".

"Oh, no, I said Trauma."

"For fuck's sake, I'm so sorry Matthew."

"You make me smile so much. Seeing you at the door last night, just, wow."

"Stop it. You're making me a flustered lady of the night."

"Tomorrow night, have dinner, somewhere up market, drink some champagne?"

"Can I get back to you on that, need to think..... Ummm, yeah ok, I'll take tomorrow night off, let's create some memories."

"You've made my day. I'll nip off to topman and get a nice shirt."

"7.30-8 ish?"

"It's a date, I mean, well, is it?"

"I guess so, is that what we call it?" Pauline holding back a bit.

"I crown this night 'date night' - for pretty Polly and the majestic Matthew."

"Oh dear lord! I'm going, see you tomorrow. Pick me up?"

"Sure will, Ciao Bella."

Pauline hangs up the phone with a smile and ponders for a minute. Maddie wheels herself to reception. "Maddie, thought you should know. Me and your father..."

"Yes, I gathered, a date was imminent."

"Ok, as long as you're ok about it, not awkward?"

"No, not at all."

"Good, because if you were you'd be fired, with immediate effect."

"What a bitch. Ugh, just think, one day you could be my step mum."

"No thanks."

Maddie snorts as she laughs too loudly. "All he bloody talked about last night was you. Polly this, Polly that. Polly put the fucking kettle on."

Pauline is secretly really chuffed inside to hear he's been talking about her. Maddie is good company to have. "Hilarious. Well, we have history and I don't think that light ever went out."

"You're telling me. The second your eyes lock it's like a candle flame, all hot and flickering away, lighting up each other's inner worlds."

"Oh shhh. Is it that obvious?"

"He didn't even look at my mum like that. The hottest he probably ever saw her was when he hauled me out of the car crash and watched her go up in a fireball."

"Maddie, that's awful. You're so dark."

"It's true though. She always wore so much Ellenette hairspray, she went up like a bomb, I mean real 'poooooffffff'. Besides, you can't get darker than living on two wheels, so fuck it, life goes on, see the funny side."

"If it keeps you positive and happy then stay in that lane Maddie. One woman's tragedy is another woman's treasure."

"I love that, that's going to be my new motto. Thanks step Mum."

"Eh, less of that, thank you."

Pauline's phone bleeps. Picks it up to read a text. "Aw, it's Layla. Says she is feeling loads better and resting and has reassessed her life. Oh, she's saying being on the game isn't for her anymore. That's a shame. I'll ring her in a minute, must be feeling low."

"You said you'd tell me about her?"

"Nothing to worry about, but she was attacked here recently and, although not her fault, she brought someone in off the street and did not book him in. From now on anyone coming through that door is on my CCTV and name in appointment book. It was an isolated incident."

"Did they find who did it?"

"No, not yet."

"Holy smoke."

"Exactly. Keep your wits about you. I've put an alarm in each room, press that and it'll make someone's ears bleed. Plus security at the door every night."

"Poor cow, that must have shaken her up."

"It did, to the core."

Leigh comes out of the bedroom looking pleased she's done her photo shoot.

"Ok, Maddie, you next. Go and strut your stuff with Ken." Maddie applies bright red lipstick, raises her eyebrow at Pauline, then exits.

Pauline rings Layla from her mobile. "Hello darling, got your message, are you ok?"

Layla is wide-eyed, hyper and sniffing and rubbing her nose, sat in a window sill, looking out at view of a park.

"All good Polly, just, you know, there is a shelf life to this game, no offence."

"None taken. Some of us just don't have an expiry date and get tastier with time, totally up to you if you feel you're all stale and no good in bed anymore."

"Touché. Wasn't getting at you, I just feel - it's time for me."

"You're broke, no place of your own, what will you do?"

Layla is shifting about and edgy. "I'll find my way. I may come back to Brighton one day and work in Waitrose, who knows."

"You're barred from there for throwing that cream pie in the cashiers face."

"Yeah well, she short-changed me. She deserved it."

"Got any retail experience?"

"Worked in a charity shop once when I came out of jail, but that years ago."

"I didn't know you did time."

"Only 5 months, for soliciting on the pavement. Felt really sorted afterwards and the last part of my sentence was on license, so I had to do volunteer work. I chose to do it in Sue Ryder charity shop."

"Ok, not quite the same, and not sure you'd wanna put that on an application form."

Layla feeling agitated. "Who cares, all in the past, who's anyone to judge me."

"I wasn't, just a bit of Momma Polly advice. So wind your neck in"

"Don't need it."

"Bet you need some money though?"

"Not really, my sis has loads of food here, I can manage. I gotta go, my sister has just come through the door." Layla is lying - she is sat in a small studio flat, alone.

"Are you sure you're ok? You sound off?"

"Yeah, yeah, all dandy. I will come visit one day, later down the line."

Pauline hesitates. "Layla, I can't say too much, but, I think I know who did this to you."

"I think I already know, no need to say it on the phone though, in case it's tapped. Let sleeping dogs lie eh."

Pauline a little startled and taken off guard. "Oh, sure, that's fine sweetheart. We will speak soon, I could drive over to see you one day." Phone goes dead and Pauline looks baffled. She knows something does not feel right about Layla.

Later Ken has finished seeing everyone and enters the lounge to say goodbye to all the girls. Pauline sees him out and thanks him with a peck on the cheek and some cash into his hand. Pauline goes back inside, where Sheila, Leigh, Sandra, Natalie, and Maddie are all in the lounge.

"Quick team meeting girls, whilst we've got a quick break in the diary. Who's staying on to do the late?"
Maddie jumps in first. "'I'll double shift, love it here."
"Me too." Natalie adds.
"Yeah I'm here all day too." Sandra replies.
"Leigh and Sandra, your turn for night off so get yourselves off and I'll see you in the morning."
Leigh is beaming.
"Been a cracking day, I felt like a model. Thanks all, see you in morning."
"Byeeeeee." Sandra waves as she exits quickly.
As they exit Pauline chats to Sheila.
"I got the flat upstairs, come up and have a look."
"That's great news, I will ring Robert to come now."

Inside the apartment upstairs, Pauline is showing Sheila and Robert around. "Great isn't it?"
Pauline points to the back bedroom.
"So, this would be your bedroom, pay some of the rent and some towards bills and we can get up and running, just need a few more working girls on the payroll and off we go."
"What a great place." Robert happily say's as he looks at Sheila.
"Yeah, better than my bedsit life, this is perfect Polly."
"Move your stuff down tonight."
"Tonight is ideal, Thank you, Polly."

"My pleasure Sheila. Oh Layla rang, she's healing happily at her sisters in Hastings, so that's nice."

"Errrmm, no she's not." Sheila corrects.

"Excuse me?"

"Polly, she's definitely not in Hastings, she was power walking along Western Road earlier, saw her from my window. Robert saw her too, I pointed her out to him."

"Yeah I saw her, well, I saw her nose first before anything else."

"Robert, don't be judgemental." Sheila embarrassed.

"No, can't be. She was on the phone to me earlier, saying she's resting and giving up being on the game."

"I've heard something else too."

Pauline getting fired up. "Go on."

"I didn't want to tell you this but, she's into coke."

"I know that, known for ages, but she's an occasional user, not some dirty coke head who's..."

Sheila is quick to tell Pauline. "Polly, she's in town and dealing coke. Someone told me she's making a mint."

"That two faced little twat, after everything I've ever done for her. I'll catch her out red-handed don't you worry. Are you sure?"

"The girl who told me bought gear off her."

"Get me an address for miss nostrils, pronto. Robert thanks for starting the door next week, I'm sure you'll settle in, but you're on probation."

"Yep, understood. I'm really grateful for this help, the least I can do is guard the doorway to your pussy kingdom."

Pauline and Sheila laugh together. "Well, I've never heard my Parlour called that before Robert."

Robert seems pleased he's made Pauline laugh. "Ha, I know, Polly's Pussy Parlour."

Pauline's eyes roll. "Ok, that's enough now, first one was funny, don't over cook it."

All three leave flat and head down the outside steps. Pauline is the last one to go down and hears a revved engine. Pauline looks over and it's Lee, sat in a car with three other men, staring at her, cold as ice. Pauline tries to look strong but can see slight worry in her eyes as she walks down the steps to the Parlour.

The girls have a busy night and Pauline has an early night, she wants to be fresh for her date tomorrow.

The following day Pauline is up early and sat out back courtyard, in white dressing gown, big cup of coffee, a cigarette and flicking through the sun newspaper. Natalie joins her with a cuppa in her hand.

A bright and breezy Natalie appears. "Morning."

"Good morning, what a stunning day for it."

"For what?"

"Treat day, then my date."

"How exciting. What are you going to wear?"

"Something new. I'm going into town and getting hair styled, sun bed, new frock and get my nails done. Had a great nights sleep too. What time did you all finish?"

"About 3 ish. It's my morning off, I may come into town with you, if that's ok?"

"Sure Nat, that'll be nice. Leigh and Sandra are doing the day shift and Lisa coming in for most of the day. Sheila in tonight"

Lisa has let herself in and comes to Pauline "Polly, I've heard something about..."

"Layla?"

"You already know?"

"I'll knock her fucking block off, good and proper. Actually no, don't want to ruin my hands, I will make my stamp on her though, one way or another."

Door buzzer goes, it's the same two police officers. Pauline's mood turns. "Well, well, well, look who it is; PC butch and PC prick on the screen." Lisa and Natalie look on, bemused as Pauline buzzes them in. PC Perry and PC Denney are whisked through to Pauline's office by Pauline.

"What do'th thee morning crow bring'th?"

PC Perry tuts and shakes his head. "Not a jovial kind of situation really Mrs Cochran." PC Perry sternly addresses her.

"Funny, now see, if my memory serves me right, you were very up for a 'funny' time the last time you walked through my doors." Pauline doesn't like his approach, so goes into attack mode, and will scrape the barrel if someone comes for her. His colleague will now know why she knows him as Graham, no shits given.

In an immensely sarcastic tone, PC Perry is quick in his response. "Then your memory doth' not serve thee right, never been here before."

Dementia isn't on my medical records PC Graham. I always know a face, especially when I've personally sat on it."

PC Perry is trying his absolute best to convince his colleague Pauline is just acting up.

"She does this to loads of people. Your defence mechanism isn't it? When you feel trapped, no way out, you'll turn the tables. Not this time, Paul."

He doesn't know Pauline well enough to know that she can be vicious. This is a line no one should cross, bringing up her past as a means of ammunition is the end of the line.

Pauline steps forward to be in his face, but still a few feet apart. PC K.D Lang puts her arm in between, thinking Pauline is going to physically lash out.

Pauline pushes her arm away and announces: "If you want to play the trans card, babe, why don't you tell your little partner here about how disappointed you were when you paid to be in my bed? How angry you were that I had fully transitioned. PC Perry here wanted a chick with a dick."

"Is there no end to your fabricated fantasy head?" He snaps. "Must be draining living in a bubble of bullshit."

Pauline's ability to recall exact details when needing to prove her honesty is undoubtedly a weapon which serves her well, especially here. With crystal clarity in her voice;

"Saturday, September 27th,1997. You walked through my doors, drunk, after the policeman's ball. You were going through a divorce and under your trousers you were wearing your wife's knickers and stockings, because you wanted to feel close to her as she had rejected you because you were firing blanks. On your right thigh you have a tattoo of the policeman's motto - Facta Non Verba."

P.C Perry looks like he wants the world to stop spinning so he can run. Pauline has her arms folded, is smirking, and in her element. Being stuck in this scenario is making the blood in his legs go cold, his colleague breaks the silence.

"I will take over from here." PC Denny takes the lead.

Pauline tilts her head back and sarcastically laughs. "Here comes the butch one, you want to make an appointment too? Bet you'd love it wouldn't you?"

"Nah, I am more into the natural woman, not an NHS slit, if you get my meaning."

Within a millisecond Pauline quips; "She says, with a gut hanging so far over her own you'd need a rescue team to haul you out if you went in there."

With no comeback, but embarrassed, PC Denny gets her professional head on.

"Pauline we have come to speak to Layla, is she awake?"

"That little trollop doesn't reside here anymore, thankfully."

"Not quite the picture you painted in interview of her. You spoke highly of her."

"Things change pretty fast in my lane. Talking of which, I have lots to do, so if you don't mind."

"Any idea where she is? This is important Pauline."

PC Denny squints at her in a sarcastic way. "After all the grief you've been through losing your lover, I'm sure you'd be happy to help."

Pauline drifts off a little and thinks, then composes herself.

"One of my girls is on it, I've asked about to find out where she is. Busy loving the white stuff and buying designer clothes no doubt."

"How would she mange that?"

"Look, I spoke with her, she sounded fucked. Then someone tells me she's back in Brighton, selling coke."

"The bag belonging to your Gary, still hasn't been retrieved."

"I know nothing about it."

"Think about it Pauline."

Pauline's eyes scan around as she's thinking. "Wait, so you think Layla is involved somehow?"

"Everyone is a suspect, until proven otherwise. Especially on a complex case like this. What's her number?"

"Here." Pauline shows her phone to them. "As soon as I find out, I will call you and update you. Let's find washed up Layla as soon as."

"Thank you. If you speak to her first tell her it's in her best interest to call in at the station."

"She's anti-law, so she won't listen to me. I will tell her though."

"Much appreciated." PC Denny's cold response.

"See yourselves out, you'll remember the way won't you, PC Graham!"

Both Police glare at her and not impressed with her attitude as they leave.

After getting ready and making sure all is in place at the Parlour, Pauline is eager to go. "Come on Nat, let's hit the shops."

"I'm cash ready, let's go." Natalie excited about getting out and being with Pauline.

Just as they step onto pavement Sheila walks towards them. "Morning double trouble."

"Hey love, last night was a laugh wasn't it?" Natalie grinning at Sheila.

"What happened? I want the goss." Pauline keen to find out.

Sheila tells her;
"We did a double booking and he wanted us to worship his cock. Like lick, kiss, suck on it, on our knees, as he was standing. Then Natalie's necklace got caught on his ball bag and she was stuck there. He was wincing as a sharp link had hooked right in. I was pissing myself, seeing her face planted into his bush and stuck there. It was hysterical."

Pauline is dying with laughter and even more so at Natalie's expression of disbelief it happened.

"Honestly, I was just stuck, and I hate hair down there, so I was gagging and all she could do was roll on the floor laughing."
Natalie half laughing, half screwing her face up with the thought.

"What did the punter do?"

"Don't know how he did it but there was a tiny bit of flesh on the chain link when he left my docking station."

"You girls make me die. We should write a book, or a TV series about what goes on, imagine that? Imagine the world seeing what really goes on for us working girls in Polly's Parlour."

Sheila takes Pauline's hand.

"Everyone should know about Polly's Parlour, it's the best place to work. Polly, I've got this for you." Sheila hands Pauline a piece of paper. "Layla's new address. Can you believe she's just around the corner? The brass neck of it. She's off her tits apparently."

"I bet she is. The police are looking for her, but don't tell her. I want to break the news to her. I need to read her face and I know her better than she knows herself."

"You didn't get it from me."

"Of course not Sheila, mum's the word. We are off shopping, see you tonight. I forgot, how was your first night in the new place?" Pauline notices a big bruise on her right arm.

"So lovely. Felt right at home, so did Robert."

"No worries at all? Things with Robert ok?"

 Making a point of staring at the bruise whilst talking."

"Oh no, that." Sheila hesitates.

"Caught it on the washing machine door."

Pauline looks like she knows there's more to the story, but not 100%, so doesn't push it.

"Music to my ears hearing you love the new home. It warms me to see you out of that bedsit. My date tonight, so off shopping for a cute outfit."

"Can't wait to see you dressed up later."

"Ok love, see you later."

"See you Ladies."

Sheila walks away, with sunken shoulders, Pauline looks back and notices. Being a Madame, she always feels it's her duty to read her girls, body language included, to ensure safety. What happened to Layla has multiplied this motherly feeling towards all the girls. She knows, her instinct and her gut feeling tells her - Robert has crossed the line. This puts Sheila to the forefront of her mind and will be on high alert. Pauline and Natalie's high heels clank in unison as they walk up the street.

Inside Selfridges' changing room Pauline has asked Natalie to go and get her a bigger size top. Whilst waiting for Natalie, in the changing room, and checking her phone, the curtain opens. Pauline's eyes pop out of her head.

"What the fuck are you doing here?"

Lee has appeared, chest puffed out, looking angry with veins in his neck popping out, and closes curtain behind him. He looks a bit like Gary when on the beach, which terrifies Pauline.

"Told ya, I am watching you and I will not stop until I recover that bag. Gary deserves to rest in peace. We had a deal going and I can't settle the debt, I need that bag."

Lee grabs her by the throat and pins her against the wall.

"Now you listen to me. Tell me who's involved and where the bag is or I will slit..."

"Lee, please, I promise you - me and Gary were fine, totally fine. I don't know what you're talking about."

"I won't ask you again. I can see it in your eyes, you know something, I'm not fucking stupid." Lee tightens his grip and Pauline turns bright red in the face.

"I am not here to play silly games, you have 5 seconds to..."

Pauline gasping for air and barely whispers..."It's Layla."

Lee loosens his grip."Who?"

Natalie returns. "Here we go, try this necklace on too, be so lovely on your date. He will love this on you."

Lee lets go of Pauline and swipes back the curtain and grabs the necklace and top.

"No thanks darlin', red ain't my colour."

Natalie stands still but stands her ground. "Who the fuck are you? You ok Polly?"

"A date Polly, already? Not so heartbroken over my brother are you? Or is this the level you hookers work on? One in and one out. Where is she Polly?"

"Who?"

"Layla?"

"This is all I have."

Pauline passes him the piece of paper out of her pocket, which Sheila gave her.

"She was one of my girls, she was attacked and then told me she was in Hastings but I found out she's back and she's high on coke and dealing. I don't know if she's connected or..."

Lee grabs the paper and storms off, on a mission. He did not need any more info, he's finally got a lead, so nothing would stop him, he's gone within three strides. Pauline sits on the floor in the changing room and Natalie sits down too, besides her.

"Is that Gary's brother?"

"Yes, he's just as vile as Gary."

"So, Layla was involved?"

"I don't know what's going on Nat, I really don't. She could be, if she's not then she can plead her case with him, it's all I had to go on."

"Try this on, don't let him ruin your day."

"I've dealt with scum like that all my life, I hope for Layla's sake she isn't guilty. The look in his eyes; blank, no emotion, apart from rage, not someone I want at my door. Thank god you came when you did, I thought he was going to strangle me to death, right here in a fucking changing room of all places."

"Let's get out of here after you try this on and get a cup of tea, come on."

Pauline cracks a small thankful smile at Natalie. "Yes, let's do that, my treat."

When the shopping trip is over Pauline attends her second therapy session with Terry.

"Welcome back Pauline, how have things been?"

"I am not great to be honest. I am involved in some heavy shit and I don't know how to keep it all together."

"Heavy shit? Can you be more specific?"

Pauline knows that if there is a possibility of threat to life, or crime, Terry is bound by a code of ethics to report it and take it out of the room, so she has made her mind up to not speak of Lee or Gary. She does not want it occupying her time in therapy.

"I want to talk about my Dad. I have been having dreams about him recently, real vivid ones. They feel real."

"What is presenting itself in the dreams?"

"Me running, but I don't get anywhere. I am trying to reach him but he gets further away and I wake up sweating and one night I woke up sobbing my heart out, from nowhere."

"What is a common occurrence amongst people having counselling is that it brings to the surface old feelings and can unlock memories and they get tangled up in our dreams. Would you like to reach out to him?"

"Nope, he can fuck off. Walked out on me and left me, I've got nothing to say to him."

"If you could, with no reply, no interference, just you being able to get it off your chest, so that you 'clear it', in a sense, what would you say?"

This has thrown Pauline. Whenever a thought about him has arisen over the years Pauline has refused to let herself think of him, so pushed it away, compartmentalised it and moved on. Being asked this question knocks the wind out of her sails and is making her think about it properly. "Why did he leave me, I want to know why it was easy to walk away and create a whole new life."

"Have you ever seen him since he left?"

"Once or twice when I was a teenager but that was back in my home town in Devon. I left at 17, never been back."

"Would you like to see him?"

Pauline looks like she is searching inside for an answer and looks peaceful.

"No, actually, no, what's the point? I've heard he's just an old boring man, full of bitterness and in an unhappy marriage. That's good enough karma for me."

"Just so I can understand properly - you feel like you want to know why he left, but you don't want to meet him. That must be confusing - to want something but to also push it away?"

"Am I fucked up in the head?"

Terry makes sure he is has certainty in his reply, he wants her to see it for exactly what it is. "You most definitely are not. You are reacting to being hurt, you are human, with a heart that feels and a mind which has imagery and memories attached, so you are bound to feel conflicted about that. You have every right to want to know why and to also be angry at him. It's what we do with it that counts. Is it effecting relationships, friendships, moods and a hindrance?"

"I feel my trust in people left with him when he drove off that day and left me with that twisted mother of mine."

"What do you feel you need to do to move on, if you are not going to see him or talk to him?"

"I guess it would be forgiveness?"

"It can be, only you would know when you open yourself up to that and see where it takes you."

"I don't want him to know I feel this, wouldn't want him to have the satisfaction."

"We can do it through meditation, visualisation or writing it out."

"I think I'm gonna need all three techniques to let this twat go."

Terry grins. "Before your next appointment I would like you to write something honest about yourself. I'd like you to direct some of it at your father and at life, let yourself be free with it."

"I'll write a poem, I've not done that for ages. I used to love writing and being creative. YES, I will do that." Pauline enthusiastically responds.

"If you'd like to get comfortable and feet on the floor, relax into the chair and let's try some visualisation. Pauline feels relaxed enough in his company and has made her mind up he's gay and has nothing to worry about. His picture of Freddie Mercury on his side board was all she needed to solidify her curiosities, so relaxes and takes deep breaths, with his guidance.

For the remainder of the session Terry shows her to look 'inside' and connect with the feelings and acknowledge them, see what she's learned from them, then an emotional release - throwing it out to the universe.

Terry has his eyes closed but opens them when he hears Pauline snoring, and leaves her to sit in that deep space for the last five minutes, and asks her to 'come back' in a very gentle voice. "Pauline, when you feel ready bring your awareness into the room and open your eyes."

Pauline seems to go the other way and her snoring becomes very pig-like. Terry has another client due, so needs her to wake up. Gently tries again. "Pauline, time to wake up."

Pauline is now leaning to the left and dribbling from the side of her mouth. Terry has no choice but to lean forward and be loud. "PAULINE, PAULINE."

This has made her jump so hard she strikes his face with her hand and is startled as she gets her bearings and is in a daze.

"Sorry, I'm so sorry. That was, erm, different." Pauline realises she's been dribbling. "Oh for fuck's sake, that's so embarrassing."

"No need, all part of the process, letting it all go."

"What, out of my mouth?"

No one has made Terry smile this much in a while.

"Not quite in that sense but..."

"Yes I know, pulling your leg aren't I."

"What did you feel when you were letting go of past issues in the visualisation?"

With a deep breath in, and blowing out of her mouth like a box fish, Pauline is holding back tears. "I had all of those feelings about my parents, let it explode and leave me. I told myself I don't need to hold onto it, it's their own journey, mine can be happy and that I wanted the anger replaced with positivity."

Terry likes what he hears. "You've done some great work again Pauline. Please be mindful that when in therapy it's not a quick fix, it will sink in, but changes take time, but I believe you're on the way to healing your pain."

Pauline thanks him and walks back to hers, in a dream like state, but with a half smile on her face. This tranquility is a new feeling, everything looks nice; the sky, the flowers, the air feels fresh, she is saying hello to every passerby when she usually wants to run everyone over. It feels like perfect timing for her. Meeting Matthew again has lifted her spirits and made her feel special, for the first time in years and years, if ever.

That evening Pauline is in her bedroom alone, finishing off her look with bright red lipstick to match her dress, looking classy, hair tonged, nails immaculate and sipping Gin & Tonic.
Sheila lets herself in.

"Hey, are you... oh my god, Polly you look gorgeous, wow. I've never seen you look so gorgeous."

"Don't I look money!"

"A million dollars."

"Why am I so nervous?"

"It's good to have butterflies, means you like him."

Door buzzer makes them both jump. "Oh sweet Jesus, he's here."

Pauline opens the door and Matthew, dressed in a crisp white shirt and navy blue trousers, sees her and his mouth widens enough to fit a tennis ball inside.

"Ah, sorry, must have the wrong building, I was looking for Polly."

"Plonker! Tah dahh, it's me."

"You look...beautiful."

"I know right?" Giggly due to the gin kicking in.

Matthew arches his arm so Pauline hold on. All the girls are stood in hallway looking happy for her.

"Give us a twirl then, Pauline." Lisa rooting for her.

Pauline does a slow spin and blows a kiss. "Bye girls, have a nice night. See you later." Pauline and Matthew leave the Parlour looking like a picture of happiness.

Pauline and Matthew are on the seafront, sitting in a dome shape glass restaurant, candles on table, sun going down out over the ocean, orange skies, calming atmosphere. Pauline and Matthew are gazing into each other's eyes.

"Seriously Polly, you are the dog's bollocks tonight."

"Charming."

"You know what I mean. Everyone looked at you when we walked in. You shine."

"Maybe they were looking at you, all George Clooney, with your salt and pepper hair."

"Hardly."

"You always were the handsome one. You've grown into yourself well with age."

"Where did it go wrong for us back then?"

"Drugs, partying, people. We were young, far too young, 18, to be tied down. Our time was great, a lovely summer fling. We had so many wonderful times and then all of a sudden I heard you were with someone else and moved away, so I just did what I do best; cracked on with my life and moved on. I always felt like you couldn't stay with me because I had not had my surgery. For years I was sad that I wasn't enough. You found that tough, didn't you?"

"Honestly? In a way yes, because I am not gay. I fell for you as a young beautiful woman. I don't like cock, I don't even like my own."

"Oh no, you're not trans as well are you?"

"This is what I loved about you - your ability to laugh at some things other people find traumatic. You have always been fearless of who you are, what you connect with and the fighting spirit you have. Are you happy Polly?"

"Now I am. You know I had my surgery a couple of years after you left?"

I did hear that once from someone but since I was out of London I lost touch with everyone. So it's true?"

"Yes. No more 'hide the sausage' jokes either."

Matthew and Pauline laugh and smile like Cheshire cats.

"I can see I was a bit angsty in my younger days. My fight was against the world, not anyone in particular. To have an internal battle going on, looking in the mirror and wishing the reflection was different, ate away at me. I started covering full length mirrors in my house and was only ever happy to look at my face. I always felt pretty, my canvas only needed a little touch up with make up, the rest was, well, a painful path. But since fully transitioning, its like a new world came to life. I see colour, feel energy, embrace nature and genuinely love my life. I still stand up against authority and anyone coming for me, that'll never change."

"And rightly so. Protecting yourself is vital. It's like there's a light on behind your eyes. I really, see you, your deeper side, you know what I am trying to say?"

"This is why I left London, to start here and leave part of my past there. I have no shame, I am proud I lived with Paul for 20 years, he was a huge part of my existence, but I am me, a human being, living my life. Gender reassignment was a process I went through to help the part of me inside which needed healing, nothing for the exterior, or acceptance, because I welcomed the real me when I was young, and that was all I needed. To be at peace with the skin I am in has enriched my soul, seriously unexpected too. I was suffocating in a masculine presence, an enemy pressing down on me. It's got nothing to do with anyone else. This woman is embracing life as the person I was meant to be."

"I am so sorry if I ever made you feel..."

"I will have none of that Matthew. We were exploring life. None of that is a mistake or a reason to apologise for. It's just life. I managed to move on, but I never stopped my feelings for you."

"So, it was easy?"

"Would it make you happy if I suffered Matthew?"

"No, of course not."

"I did though, deep inside."

"I'm so sor...."

"Nope, don't want an apology. You did what you had to do."

"I felt trapped really. Maddie's mum was a bit of a psycho and fell pregnant after one night, it wasn't meant to be like that."

"But it did, and you have Maddie. She's a chip off the old block, a real entertainer, just like you used to be."

"I needed drugs to be as wild as her, she's on another planet. But I wouldn't change a thing."

"Glad to hear it. You see Matthew, it was meant to be, it just wasn't our time then."

"So you're saying this is our time?"

"Maybe, who knows, we're here now aren't we?"

Waitress approaches and interrupts the chat. "Ready to order?"

Pauline and Matthew realise they haven't even looked at the menu and without even looking Matthew replies; "She will have the prawn cocktail to start, followed by medium cooked steak with salad and chips, a G & T, and I'll have the same."

"You remembered, after all this time."

"How can I forget when you dropped those dripping prawns down your cleavage that time."

"Ok, waitress doesn't need to hear this."

Waitress blushes and walks off to kitchen.

"You have got a good memory, that was in that restaurant up on

St. James' Street wasn't it?"

Matthew takes her hand and looks into her eyes. "Yes, our first date that was. This feels like a first date again too."

"Maddie says she can see it between us."

"She knows me well and she likes you, she approves. So what do you say to date 2, 3, 4 - maybe more?"

"You're a poet all of a sudden. I'm sure I could squeeze you in for another date, we'll see."

Matthew's smile lights up his face. "We will, I know it." Matthew kisses her hand. "I never stopped loving you Polly."

Pauline's breath is taken away and puts her hand on her chest and her eyes well up.

"No one has ever said that to me."

"What, never? In all these years?"

"Nope, just fists and broken promises."

Waitress places their drinks on table and walks away.

"Tell the past to piss off Polly, I've got you, ALWAYS."

Pauline has a slight tear in her eye and smiles.

"Thank you, Matthew, that means a lot. Let's see where it takes us. I believe we are where we are meant to be in each other's lives, in whatever form that may be."

Pauline raises her glass.

"To us."

Matthew raises his.

"To us."

CHAPTER SIX

Cocaine

Life is looking vibrant for Pauline the past few days. Polly's Parlour 2 has opened, the girls have been doing double shifts as punters are rolling in. Pauline needs more girls and has some lined up, knowing the money is rolling in is just what she needs. Matthew has been beautiful to her, roses sent to door, texting her every morning. She's been radiating because of it and everyone can see it.

The only gripe she has, is with Robert. She was right not to fully invest in him, but to keep him close, so she could figure him out. Pauline has heard shouting and this morning, seen Sheila quickly go into the apartment upstairs with sunglasses on, which she's never seen before.

Pauline was told this morning by Leigh that Sheila has confided in her that he's beaten her but she's too scared to tell Pauline, in case it makes it worse. Inside Pauline is raging and only needs to hear something like that once for her to take action. No one will hurt one of her girls, not on her watch. At this moment she cannot sort anything as she has to go out, with Lisa, just for an hour or two.

Lee has been off the scene so Pauline feels on edge again when Lee decides he wants a celebration party for Gary's life, even though the funeral will be soon. Pauline feels this it's a bit odd, but accepts the invitation.

It's held at a prestigious hall in a 5-star hotel, with chandeliers, champagne and caviar. Lee is strutting around, suited and booted, and has clearly had too many flutes of champagne. Pauline is trying to stay low-key and at the sides, and has managed to avoid him for over an hour. With her back to the room, Pauline is chatting quietly to Lisa.

"Don't think much of this spread, do you Lisa?"

"Never liked fish, so no desire to eat their eggs. I've had more satisfaction from a 20p mix up."

"You've had fish and chips before now."

"That's totally different because of the batter and, ah, Lee's coming this way." Lisa's body language shows she is not liking the view.

Pauline doesn't look round and swigs some champagne, for dutch courage. As Lee approaches her he starts whacking his glass with a knife, pulls Pauline's arm so she turns to face him, and the room. Very loudly Lee addresses the room.

"Can I have everyone's attention please." Another loud tapping of the glass.

"Lee, please." Pauline quietly pleads.

The room falls silent, waitresses with their canapé's stand still, the bar staff stop serving, all eyes are on Lee and Pauline.

"Everyone this is Pauline, or as some men like to call her "Polly", Gary's last lover, isn't that right, Polly?"

Pauline puts on a brave face, stands tall and half smiles.

"So, surely, this grieving girlfriend of my dead brother has a few words to say, don't you?"

Pauline manages to push a tear out and wipes it. "I don't think this is the right time Lee, I'm too upset to..."

"Nonsense. We would all love to hear from you, wouldn't we, everyone?" Lee's tone turning creepy. Some guests look uncomfortable, some nod, others sip a drink. One waitress scoffs a snack off of her tray. Lee stumbles as he grabs Pauline and puts his arm around her.

"Come on Darling, for Gary, just a few words."

Composing herself she gets the courage to put on her best act.

"Thank you, Lee. As much as it hurts to lose Gary, it's a real comfort to see so many people come to celebrate his life. I know he would have loved this and would have meant the world to him. And Lee, thank you for being there for me." Lee glares at her, but lets her finish.

"Gary treated me like a lady and showed me so much love in his final days." Few frowns, looks of confusion, not quite the Gary people seem to recall.

"Wherever you are now babe, rest in peace." Pauline raises her glass. "To Gary." The whole room lift glasses and in unison "To Gary."

The room noise starts as people mutter and start moving again. Lee holds her wrist tightly, without anyone seeing. Lisa stood in fear but trying to look calm.

"Listen to me, Polly, we've got unfinished business."

"I've told you, I don't know where the coke is." Pauline is panicking now, she wants out of this situation, out of this family, her head is frazzled, but keeping it together.

"I'm sorting that."

"You mean you're sorting Layla out? Do you know where she is?"

"Never you mind. Leave her to me. I am closer to the missing bag, I can feel it."

Lee is acting differently, he seems weird, like he is vacant behind the eyes, on a mission, in the zone, hard to put a finger on it as an outsider looking in.

Pauline doesn't know him well enough to know what he is doing, or planning. What she feels strongly about is Layla would not kill someone, even if they hurt her. It doesn't sit right with her.

Pauline gives him a supportive and kind approach.

"Lee, I don't think it was Layla."

Pauline is feeling guilty that she may be innocent and does care for her deep down, so makes up a lie.

"Layla was out of town that night Gary was killed, at some rave my mate was at. I was told that this morning. I double-checked for you and saw some photos they took."

"She knows something, my gut is telling me. Who do you think did it eh? Who the fuck did my brother over?"

In the moment Pauline blurts out;

"Robert, a northern twat, just moved in above my place. He's not right in the head. Arrived on the scene few days before Gary was killed."

"Who's he living with?"

"I've no idea, he's random. He showed up looking for a room to rent and hanging around, asking questions."

"What kind of questions?"

"He mentioned Gary one day but I brushed it off and said I didn't know him as I knew Gary didn't like being talked about, so I respected his privacy. Just find him a bit, I don't know, weird is the word."

"Did he now, that's dodgy. What flat number above you?"

"Directly above, 48b. He's seeing a lovely girl called Sheila, keep her out of this, she's a doll and he's given her a good hiding before now. He's nasty work."

"Right, I will be having some alone time with him imminently. Don't breathe a word of this to anyone."

"I don't say shit to anyone, I like my privacy, that's why me and your brother clicked"

Lee looks at her deeply, with his boozy glassy eyes.

"You know, maybe, just maybe, I've had you all wrong. So far you've been there, and I've not found a fault, and trust me I can find them. Either that or you're one very clever chick. An actress in a previous life perhaps."

Pauline's shoulders drop, the tension in her subsides a little, she smiles and looks into his eyes. "If only I was, but I'm not. I was kicked out of School and own a brothel, hardly sign of a clever chick."

"She is clever." Lisa adds. Pauline's head almost spins off as she fiercely turns to Lisa, wondering what the hell she is going to say next. Lisa stumbles. "I mean, you know, clever as in - able to drive, I've never passed, I'm so dumb."

"Hey, don't put yourself down like that, I know a good driving instructor I could hook you up with - mates rates an all that." Lee offers.

"Ah that would be lovely, yes..."

Pauline cuts Lisa up and glares at her. "She doesn't want to drive, she's had too much champagne Gary, I mean Lee, sorry, God."

"It's ok, people have always got our names the wrong way round. Thank you for coming, it does mean a lot. I would love to hear about your little love story with my brother. He was a brute to people, including women, that's why it is so unbelievable that he was nice to you."

"Like I said, it was only a month, but it was a beautiful month."

"Still, I'd like to hear it from you."

"She was always happy when coming back from being with Gary, always." Lisa says meaningfully.

"Let's get you home young lady. Lee, it's been a lovely day, you did him proud."

Lee gently takes her hand and gives her a kiss on the cheek and hands her his card. "And you've done me proud. Take my number, in case you need anything. Put it in your phone."

Pauline smiles, punches the number into her phone and sends him a text, then takes Lisa's hand. "You have mine now too. Bye Lee, take care of yourself."

Pauline and Lisa exit, as Lee cries into a tray of Vol -Au-Vents.

Later that day, Pauline and Lisa enter Polly's Parlour and can hear noises coming from a bedroom, so listen outside the door and can hear Sandra.

"I said kneel the fuck down you little bitch, now follow me."

As the door swings open, they see Sandra in a leopard print catsuit, with a black basque over the top, long chain in one hand, leading an old slave, about 40 years old, who is crawling along the floor behind her, naked.

"Ooops sorry, please, go on through." Pauline welcomes him with smile.

Sandra smirks at Pauline as Sandra heads off towards the kitchen with slave.

"Right, come on, you've got a kitchen to scrub clean."

"Yes Mistress, yes." The slave whimpers.

Adding a dominant demand into the mix, Pauline yells; "Do the oven whilst you're at it."

"Yes Madame Polly."

"Good boy, I will be inspecting it later, so it better be up to my standards."

Sandra steps in. "Um, he can make me some chips first, I'll sit and eat whilst he's cleaning." Slave looks up at Sandra as though this isn't part of the deal. Sandra, with widened eyes, screams at him, "Did I say you can look at me?"

"No, sorry Mistress, please punish me."

Sandra whips him with the chain as he yelps as they enter the kitchen and close the door.

"I could do with him coming round to mine, it's a tip." Lisa yawns.

"Doesn't your mother clean?"

"Nope, not lately anyway."

"Why not?"

"She's back on the gear again. I've seen more energy in someone on a life support machine. She's spaced out and lays there all day."

"You can't live like that, why didn't you tell me? That's really sad Lisa. Is this why you've slept here some nights?"

"Yeah, I'm sorry I just...." Lisa starts to cry.

"No need to be sorry darling. You haven't done anything wrong. Are you paying for her habit?"

"Yeah, sadly. But the rent is paid by the council, so I get free rent. I just feel sorry for her, she's my mum, I love her, so I give her money."

"Enabling an addict isn't love, it's done with love but it's also a bad habit, a vicious circle. You'll move in here and I won't have a word said about it. Low rent and extra pay when you want to slip off reception and into working girl mode. You cannot live like that. You need a plan of action."

"I don't want to do punters anymore. I'm not versatile enough."

"You've done it loads of times. Lisa, this denial is endearing but it's ok to like having sex for money. I would never ever force you to do it, but you've got a gift. Men always want you when they meet you."

"Do they? Aww that's sweet. But, I love being on reception and chatting to them all."

"And that's fine too, just, don't place yourself off of the menu. Men will pay for your chats in a sexual way and maybe some dominatrix work, like Sandra does. There's no sex, you just gotta be confident and ballsy, save up for the future."

Lisa deep in thought. "I will think about it. Thank you, Polly, I'm so grateful. Are you sure about moving in?"

"Yes, pop home and pack some things and have a chat with your mum. You need to break the cycle and your mum will have to fight her own battles from now on. You've done a lot for that woman."

"You're right. I will walk there now and fill a taxi with some of my stuff. This is a good chance for me isn't it?"

"Sure is darling, you need think of yourself for a change. Now hurry up and get back asap."

"Will do. Shall I check on Sheila first?"

Thuds heard on floor upstairs and glass smashing. Lisa looks scared. Pauline looks like she is about to go to war; rolls up her sleeves, kicks her heels off and puts on a pair of boots.

"No, you go. I will go and see her now and sort that dickhead out, run along and I will see you soon."

Pauline lets herself in the front door of Polly's Parlour 2, and sees Robert swigging neat whiskey and some broken glass on the floor.

"Where's Sheila?"

"Let yourself in why don't you."

"I will. It's my fucking flat, where is she? Sheila?" Pauline yells louder - "SHEILA?"

"Be there in a sec, just on the loo."

"Ok I'll be here, waiting."

Robert's eyes are dead, nothing like they were before. His true colours are evident amongst his alcohol breath. "She doesn't need mothering."

"You're right, she doesn't, or smothering , but needs protecting."

"From?"

Pauline looks him up and down as he swigs a mouthful.

"You, look at you, what a mess. You've just lost tonight's shift."

"What? I didn't ask for a night off. I'm supposed to start my first shift in a few hours."

"You don't need to ask, I'm telling you. You will not be working my door tanked up with cheap whiskey inside you." Pauline notices a large amount of white powder in a see through bag on the side, but does not let him know she has seen it. "If you've laid a finger on her."

Just as Robert is about to reply, Sheila walks in, all light and breezy, with a spring in her step, wearing big sunglasses and a huge, yellow, floppy summer hat on.

"Migraine?" Pauline sarcastically asks.

"Pardon?"

"The sunglasses, what's with them on indoors?"

"I'm just on my way out into the sun."

"It's raining. Come here."

Sheila hesitantly walks towards Pauline. Pauline swipes the sunglasses off. Sheila has a black eye and one blood shot eye. Pauline turns to Robert.

"Jesus, you vile bully. Sheila go down stairs to mine."

Robert stands up and looks furious. "I don't fucking think so."

"You don't bark orders at me you prick, don't forget this is my gaff. Now, back the fuck up and sit back down in your misery."

Robert lunges for her and stumbles. Pauline swings her arm back like she is bowling in a cricket championship match and punches him right on the nose. A loud crack brings this meeting to a close as Robert falls to the ground.

Pauline puts one boot into the gut.

"And *that* is for all the women you've hurt."

Pauline grabs Sheila's arm and they both leave to go back down to Polly's Parlour. Pauline texts Lee en route.

In a dark lounge, with curtains closed, music pumping, Layla is sat on a chair with her legs and hands taped together with gaffer tape, with marks all over her. She is in and out of consciousness and has taken a battering, her second in two weeks. Layla can hear quite a bit of what is being said but will not open her eyes.

Snorting lines and drinking Hennessy, are two men, Lee and his mate Darren.

Lee is totally fucked up and spinning out about knowing Layla not having anything to do with Gary's death, but the drugs he's been taking means he's got a paranoid fixation in his head that she definitely knows something about the coke. He is not ready to let her go as he knows she takes coke and she's been selling it, he thinks. If he lets her go and finds out she knows something, then he would forever hate himself. This isn't something Lee is willing to allow into his life. The chances of Layla making it out are slim. Lee is falling about with white powder over his nostrils and a gurning face.

"Rack up some more lines mate, I'm just getting more ice."

As Lee takes ice out of fridge and walks past Layla, he throws ice over her head, so she starts to stir a little and half opens her eyes.

"Chin chin, Layla."

"Man, that's funny as."

"Crank that tune up Darren."

Darren turns the music up so the room is vibrating, stirring Layla even more.

"Mate, you just said my real name, for fuck's sake man."

"You didn't think she's getting out of here alive anyway did you?" Lee laughs hard.

Darren suddenly looks like he's seen a ghost and displays panic in his body language.

"What? I thought this was for a few days until she opens up and tells us where the coke is?"

"Nah, nah, she's seen our faces now, too late."

Lee looks serious. As Darren sits on the arm of the sofa and thinks.

"The look on your face mate, that plan has changed course. I know she didn't kill Gary."

Lee starts to get upset and holds it in, but is struggling. Lee takes it out on Layla and slaps her around the face.

"But I do believe you have been involved with the white goods, somehow, just a hunch. So, conk nose, want some more powder?"

Through slurred speech Layla manages to speak. "No, please. I've told you I don't know anything."

Darren holds his chest and looks like he's spinning out.

"What's up mate?"

"Dunno, been getting these pains on and off all week."

"Ha, it's this Ketamine mate, this is top grade shit, enjoy it, embrace it." Lee lights a joint and blows smoke circles. "Come on, let's do more."

As Darren cuts up more lines on the glass table Lee walks towards Layla and pulls her hair back and rubs some Ketamine into her gums.

"Come on Layla, open wide, time to confess, I'm getting bored now. Mate, I'll have to give her more."

"More? How did you get her to snort a line?"

"There're other holes to ram powder into you know."

"Wow, that's deep man."

Layla pleads. "Please, I need the toilet."

Lee is frustrated and impatient and drags her to the toilet and undoes her hands, keeps feet taped, pulls her skirt down and sits her on the bathroom toilet, stands by the door - keeping watch. As Layla is peeing Lee gets a text which reads, "He's home alone" from Pauline. Lee's eyes light up like he's won the lottery,

"Finished." Layla calls out.

Lee drags her back to chair in lounge, sits her down and tells Darren he has to go out.

"Don't you need me there?"

"Nope, too many looks suspicious, I can manage this one, keep your eye on this one. She's out of it, sure you can handle her. Put some more tape around her hands."

Darren looks as though he doesn't know what day of the week it is, let alone take an order and stick to it.

"Here have this line before you go."

Both snort one and cheer, high five and Lee leaves in a hurry. Darren has never been higher than he is at this moment, this is serious gear. Layla pretends to fall asleep, tilting her head to the side, but watches him dance around to house music through one half open eye. Darren dances like he's an air traffic controller and talking as if there are people with him - he's tripping in a psychedelic world. Soon Darren begins to hold his chest again, tries to catch his breath, bends over for a minute and tries to get himself together. But, his chest seems to hurt more, falls over on the floor clutching his chest and gasping for breath.

Layla struggles immensely for what feels like an eternity, but manages to undo the tape around her legs, with her hands. Layla walks over to Darren, who's gasping for air and begging for help, face bright red. Layla spits on him then leaves the apartment out of the back door and out of a gate, stumbling and falling, but escapes down an alleyway.

Lisa puts her key in the front door at her mum's house and hears noises and commotion. Lisa enters the lounge to see two men in balaclavas, with a knife to her mother's throat.

"Noooo, please, that's my mum."

Lisa explains as she enters this mayhem. One of the men takes Lisa by the collar and pushes her down next to her mother. Lisa's mum is out of it; eyes rolling and has a needle in her arm.

"What have you done to her?" Lisa stares into both their eyes, a look of coldness.

"Mommy dearest did this to herself, and she owes us big bucks."

"What? I give her some of my money daily, how can she be in

debt?"

"Look at her. She isn't a £40 a day habit kind of bird."

Lisa is shaking and out of her depth. "I'll pay it off. What is it, like, 300-400? Here I've got some in my purse, I can pay now."

Both men howl with laughter as the one man communicating with her snatches her handbag and empties it on the floor and takes what she has, around £40. "Add a couple of zero's sweetheart."

"Four grand?"

"Spot on. Was two but it's just gone up. Interest rates are high."

Lisa panic-stricken, looks at her mum, tears in her eyes. "I'll get it, I swear I can get it, just give me some time, please."

"You've got one week. No payment means no mummy, dead, gone." Man makes gun shot sign with fingers as they leave out of the back door.

Lisa gently takes the needle out of her mum's arm and cradles her in tears. "Mum, please, this has to stop." As Lisa looks deep into her mum's eyes, the lights are on but she's not home. Cold sad eyes, in and out of sleep state. "I know you're in there, mum, I need to help you. But I just need to go away for a few days and get the money." Mum does not react, not even a flicker. Lisa sobs and rocks her mum in her arms.

Inside Polly's Parlour, Pauline and Sheila enter the office, only to see Maddie on the bed dressed as an old milkmaid; blonde wig, blue and white bonnet with frills.

"Oh, Maddie, I didn't know you were on shift today?"

"Yeah Polly, I'm milking a cow today, well Colin, but you know."

"That's a first, cute little outfit may I say."

Maddie see's Shiela's face. "God, Sheila, what's happened?"

"I walked into..." Sheila about to make up a lie.

Pauline interrupts and decides to be transparent in this

situation. "A fist is what she walked into. Right, we will get out of your way, good luck."

"Mooooooooo." Maddie breaks the tension with the sound just as a punter, Colin, comes out of the bathroom door dressed in a cow costume, embarrassed.

Pauline greets him.

"Welcome to Polly's dairy farm, please, go on through to the milking station.' Colin scuttles into the 'farm'.

Sheila and Pauline head to go out to back yard for a break. They go through the lounge, into the kitchen, where slave is washing dishes. Food is in the oven and Sandra has her feet up on the table, applying nail varnish to her toes.

"Really? On my dining table?"

"My feet are clean, he's just licked them all over, every crease."

"Put some tissue down, I don't want your hoofs on my mahogany. And tell him to make a pot of tea for me and Sheila."

"Oiii, slave. Make a brew, put some biscuits on a plate, and hurry up."

"Yes Mistress."

Pauline and Sheila sit down outside. Pauline lights up a cigarette and looks confused as Sheila helps herself to one out of her packet and lights it up.

"Excuse me?"

"Sorry, I should have asked."

"No, it's not about taking one, it's about having one. You don't smoke."

"Today I do."

"What did he do?"

"It was a one off."

Pauline takes Sheila's hand and gazes into Sheila's eyes.

"Darling, I've not been around the block, multiple times, not to see the signs. I could tell by your face this morning. I knew something was off about him. How many times has he struck you?"

"Once up in Leeds and once down here, that's all, honestly. I could be to blame as he says I flutter my eyelashes too much at other men when we are out socialising."

"Fanny wobbles, clap trap. Think he would give a shit about that, when you sell sex for a job?"

"That's what I said. But he said that's work and, apparently, I do it to all men we are around."

"Sweetheart, that's guilt dialogue, transference of his internal insecurities, trust me, I've met many like that. It'll never stop - the power struggle, the jealousy, the black eyes. I can see it in him, he's a lost little boy punching his way through life, trying to figure it all out. You will never change that, you're not his therapist or his padless sparring partner."

"I know, I know. I'm embarrassed and ashamed. You always speak the truth but he's here now, what can I do?"

"Never ever be ashamed, you've done nothing wrong. He came here to just try and take you back? Nah, that doesn't sit well with me. He probably ran here, I doubt no one even knows where he is - which would make it easier for him to disappear. I bet my life on it. Leave this to me. You are having pamper night; face pack, bubble bath, candles, relaxation music. You need this tonight."

"That's so kind. Will I be able to put my cut into the bath though?"

"What cut?"

"Here, where he smashed a pint glass at my head." Sheila lifts the side of her hair up and reveals a small gash. Pauline looks at it closely.

"That fucking low life. We need the first aid kit, I think it's minor, won't need stitches. Let me clean this up for you."

"The kit is in the office though."

In the back ground they hear noises coming from the 'farm yard'.

"Arrgghhh, yes, yes, take 6 pints from my udders please little milky milk maid."

"This is the best full fat I've ever tasted in my life. Whoohhh whoooo."

Sheila laughs, Pauline looks pleased to see her smiling.
"You'll be ok kid, as long as I draw breath, you'll be ok."

Loud banging and kicking to the front door, leads Pauline to the intercom, to look on camera - it's Robert, stumbling and shouting.

"Sheila, fucking get out here now, I'm taking you back to Leeds."

Pauline picks up the intercom. "Over my dead body you'll take her, now piss off before I call the Police."

"Bitch." Robert gives door one more kick, then stumbles back up to flat above and doesn't close the door properly, too drunk to even notice, or care.

Lisa pulls up in taxi, mascara running down her face, two bin liners full and a ruck sac on her back. Pauline buzzes her in.

"What's with the tear stains? Was it that tough saying goodbye, it's only temporary darling."

"I nearly had to, for real, say goodbye, forever."

Lisa starts to sob in the hallway, lowers her bin liners, sits on them, with head in her hands. Pauline crouches down and puts her arm around her and wipes her face with tissue.

"Eh, eh, eh, come on Lisa, this isn't like you. You're always full of the joys of spring. What's the matter?"

Catching her breath and composing herself, Lisa grips Pauline's arm.

"There were two men, in balaclavas, at my mum's, wanting to kill her as she owes them four bloody grand."

"For what?"

"She's back on heroin, yet again, and I've said I'll pay."

"You said what?"

"They were going to slit her throat, I'm telling you, they meant it. I've got one week to raise it."

"Who are they?"

"Dealers I suppose."

"Where have you got to go to pay them?"

"Back home, in one week."

"You're just going to sit there and wait for them to arrive? Because you can't leave it with your mother."

"Pauline, you should have seen the state of her - eyes glazed over and a needle hanging out of her arm."

Sheila looking sad for her.

"Oh no, that's so sad. She looked so well when we bumped into her a couple of months ago in town."

"She was trying, she always tries, but always fails. I can't let them kill her, she's my mum."

"That's not going to happen. We can sort this. Remember what we spoke about this morning, about branching out? Turn this sadness and frustration into a character, use it to make this money."

"What were you speaking about this morning?"

"Dominatrix, no sex, just making good money from slaves and ..."

Mid flow they all notice Colin stood in hallway in his cow outfit, with a pint glass bottle half full of milk, with some milk in his goatee beard, looking a picture of sympathy for Lisa.

Pauline, Sheila and Lisa burst out laughing.

"Sorry, Colin, it's just, we didn't expect a cow to be standing there."

With his Somerset farmer accent, "It's fine Polly, I know it's an udderly odd thing to see, however, I couldn't quite help over-hear."

Maddie wheels herself into the hallway too, then the slave crawls behind Sandra as she appears.

"Crikey, look at it all; a Madame, a dominatrix, a cow, a slave, a bruised girl and..."

"Yeah go on, you can say it." Maddie calmly encourages Pauline.

"I was actually about to mention Lisa's mascara face, then call you a cripple, because I know you love that word so much. Sorry, Colin, you were saying?"

"I may be able to help, financially."

Lisa perks up. "Really? Colin, thank you so much."

"You'll have to work for it."

"Oh!" Lisa's hope for a free cash injection wiped out.

Pauline nudges Lisa. "How lovely of him isn't it Lisa? What kind of work are you proposing to my girl?"

"Outdoors mainly, at my parents' old farm. They have unused outdoor space as we don't have animals anymore, so I'd like to explore all animal scenarios." Turns to Maddie. "No offence, but, well, the access isn't wheel worthy."

"Never really been an animal lover anyways, don't even eat them. So you crack on Lisa, go and get the piggy pounds. Oink oink." No one laughs. "Ok, great, I'll slip off and get ready for my surgeon."

Colin shocked. "Surgeon?"

"Yeah, I have to pretend to be a patient as he fiddles about and I flat line so he can revive me, a few times. Like a hero, the saviour of the day. Dr Resuscitate."

"Wow, you really are multi talented. Polly, she is great you know, knows her stuff. I'm very pleased with today's, err, deposit."

"We aim to tease and always please."

"I love that. We should get that made into a sign. Colin, thank you, can I get back to you." Lisa replies.

Pauline supports her. "She's been through a lot today, let her sleep on it. If not Sandra will step in won't you Sandra?"

Colin looks horrified. "Um, yeah, thanks all the same, it's just that I'm looking for, young off spring farm animals, if you get my meaning."

This gets Sandra's back up. "You cheeky little..."

"That's enough thank you." Pauline quickly killing that sentence. "Back to the kitchen please. Is my oven clean yet slave?"

"Almost Madame Polly."

"Off you crawl then."

Sandra leads him away, Colin goes to bathroom, Maddie shuts bedroom door. Pauline turns to Lisa and Sheila. "They can work double shifts today and Leigh & Natalie will be in later, you two are having a well deserved night off. Lisa, you've got a lot to think about."

"I once played a donkey in the school nativity, I could draw on that I suppose."

"It's gonna need a lot more groundwork than that my lovely. Why don't you do face packs, a little snooze in your new bedroom and go to the cinema or to a bar, recharge yourselves?"

"What a great idea. Come on Lisa, let's go to the cinema and eat lots of sweets and popcorn."

"Sure. I need a rest first, I am so drained."

"That's my girls." Pauline pulls out her purse and hands them some cash. "Here, this one is on me."

"No, it's ok I, actually, my handbag is upstairs with Robert." Sheila annoyed at herself.

"Thanks Polly, really appreciate this."

"It's no bother, it'll do you both the world of good. You've worked back to back shifts and been through a lot. Go and be young and have fun."

Just as Colin is leaving he hands Lisa a card with his number on it. "Don't forget it's an outcall, so I pay extra for that as well. Call me tomorrow?"

"Thank you, Colin, I will give it some serious thought."

Colin leaves and just as Lisa is heading to the bathroom door there are loud thuds, noises and things being smashed coming from Polly's Parlour 2 above.

"What the hell is that?" Lisa stands still to listen more.

"Must be Robert in a rage and kicking off, to himself probably, freak." Sheila adds.

"Something like that yes. Let's put some music on." Pauline presses play on stereo at reception and 'Livin' La Vida Loca' blares out, Pauline starts to dance and sing along.

Maddie comes out of bedroom in wheelchair, in a blue hospital gown. "Oh my gawwwddd, I looove Ricky Martin, he is so my type."

"Yeah, umm, I don't think you're his type though."

"Wow, what a bitch - just because I'm on wheels?"

"Bless you, no, just a hunch that's all. Let's dance."

Pauline, Sheila and Lisa start to dance and Pauline grabs Maddie's chair and spins her around too fast. Maddie flies out of the chair onto the floor, banging her head, they all laugh loudly as Maddie is in hysterics, drowning out the noise upstairs.

Sheila and Lisa are dolled up and ready to go out, Sandra is in bathroom, Maddie is under sedation, or rather pretending to be. Natalie is dressed as an elf, next to Leigh, whom is sat on the front desk in a Christmas outfit; tinsel all over, sparkly make up, lights in her hat, red fishnets, mini Santa outfit, holding a wrapped up present. Pauline comes out of her bedroom and sees them and looks baffled

"You two, it's Summer."

"We are doubling up for some festive fun." Natalie seems happy to be in the outfit.

"Why?"

"Don't ask me, a client rang and said he wanted some fun on yule tide, so here I am. Ho ho"

"Girls have a lovely time and bring me back some popcorn please."

"We will, see you all later. Byyyeeeee." Sheila seems brighter.

As they leave a punter enters; Geoff, 20s, thin frame, goatee beard and nervous.

"Evening darling, Mrs Christmas is perched and ready." Pauline announces happily.

Geoff thinks he's heard wrong, "Sorry, excuse me?"

Natalie is holding a lit Christmas pudding on a tray, Leigh is full of herself and looking festive, all lit up with a huge grin, selling it wholeheartedly to Geoff; "Jingle bells my lovely, here I am. Where's the reindeer?"

"I don't understand, it's August. Why the outfit?"

"Errmm, because you said 'fun on yule tide'. So, tah dah."

"Oh, this is awkward. I said "fun on your thighs."

"What? I could have sworn..."

"Must have been a bad line. Girls go and change please, Sir, come through to the lounge."

"What about my thighs anyway, what do you want with them?"

"I want them wrapped around my neck, wrestle me with them. I need to be dominated."

"That's easy, I used to do judo as a kid, I will take you down babe."

"I may be thin but I am strong. I don't want it to be easy, I want the challenge. You said on the phone you're strong and tough."

"Yep, that's me." Leigh flexes her muscles and Geoff looks paralysed with excitement. Leigh and Natalie get changed, the rest go to the lounge.

The Slave is putting on his coat and is back into his normal clothes. Slave has his wallet out and hands a £20 note to Pauline.

"What's this for?"

"I couldn't help but overhear your conversation earlier. Can you add this to her funds please? It's not much but..."

"Ah that's so sweet of you, yes she really is a kind soul." Pauline feels uneasy. "What did you over hear exactly?"

"Just that she needs 4 grand."

"Nothing else?"

"No, honestly, just that."

"Ok, well, thank-you. See you next week?"

"Umm, yeah, can I have a word, just between me and you please?"

"Sure, are you ok Slave?"

"It's ok you can call me by my real name when I'm out of the harness." He whispers.

"Oh right, I don't recall you telling me."

"It's Teddy."

Pauline laughs. "Aww, named after a cuddly teddy bear?"

"No, Ted Bundy."

"OH. What can I help you with?"

"It's about Miss Dominatrix. I'm not sure if I should tell you this but.."

"Go on..."

"She needs to lay off the carbs."

"Come again?"

"Flatulence, not just a mild breeze either. It's putting me off a little, but I cannot talk to my superior like that."

"Right, leave that with me. I'm sure it can be..."

"It's not just that. You see, when I booked I was told she was in her twenties."

"Oh we all shave a bit off Teddy, makes it more youthful and appealing to most."

"I'm not most unfortunately, she's closer to my mum's age I should imagine."

"Teddy, that's unkind. But I may have a solution. Lisa may be 'branching out' you see."

Teddy salivates. "Really? Oh my giddy aunt, I feel like I need to sit down."

"Are you in shock? What's going on?"

"Polly, I know I've only been here three times but when I first came here and Lisa was sat at the desk, my eyes lit up as I thought she was my mistress, then you brought out." Points behind.

"Do you have a number I can call you on?"

"I'm afraid only my home number but my Mum may answer, so best not."

"Work phone?"

"I'm a copper, so..." Stunned silent stare from Pauline. "Don't worry, when I'm off duty I'm not interested. I can call you from a call box if you can schedule that in somewhere?"

Pauline flicks through diary. "How about tomorrow 6pm?"

"Yes. Definitely."

"Ok that's in the diary Teddy, let Polly work her magic.

"Thank you, Polly, you really are the best in the business."

"I've grafted and earned my stripes in this game of sexual desires. Brothels are where the tension, aggression, sadness and joy can all be off loaded, which makes the world a better place in my eyes."

"When you put it like that - yes. May I ask you a personal question?"

"I'm an open book, fire away."

"You deserve a nice man, someone to take care of you. You look after us men, I'd like to think someone has your back too."

"Ah, Teddy, that's one of the nicest things anyone has ever said. Thank you. And, yes, I have met someone and taking it steady. Met years ago and then rekindled recently and so far so lovely."

"If ever you need me to look anyone up on the data base, or anything to keep you safe, if I can do it I will."

"You're a sweet gentleman, thank you."

"Well, I hope this man respects you."

"I feel he's a keeper, but we shall see. Speak to you tomorrow at 6 then."

"Yes, look forward to it."

Pauline buzzes him out and the home phone rings. "Good evening, Polly's Parlour."

"Hello my gorgeous specimen of a lady."

Pauline blushes and acts coy.

"Whoooh, get you calling me your lady. That sounds fancy."

"Fancy you don't I? Can't help it. My little Polly pocket."

"Ok, go easy on the metaphors my love."

"Whooh, get you calling me your love."

"Oh give over you. Anyway, what do I owe this honour?"

"Obviously wanted to hear your voice and to ask how Maddie is?"

"She's fine, about to go under the knife."

"Wait, whaattt?"

"Relax, it's just some role play stuff."

"That worries me. Not in a sadistic way I hope?"

"God, no, think more 'Hospital Hero' vibe."

"Right, um, I'd rather not think of anything at all."

"Then don't ask. She is fine here under my roof and I have security on my door at nights."

"I know, just a worrier aren't I?"

"You always were. Nothing wrong with looking out for others - it's a lovely quality."

"I guess so."

"Weather is so lovely, fancy a picnic tomorrow?"

"I know just the place. Pick you up 9am?"

"Steady on, let a lady wake up and give the puffiness enough time to simmer down."

"You do make me chuckle. Ok see you at 9.30?"

"No, make it 11."

"Jesus. Ok, 11am it is. Mwah mwah."

"See you then. MWAH MWAH."
Pauline hangs up with a huge smile on her face. Sandra comes out dressed as a nurse with a small silver tray, with a syringe and small bowl and cotton wool on.

"What's this I see before me."

"Good evening. I am the anaesthetist for today." Sandra professionally responds.

"Of course you are." Pauline receives a text from Lee saying, "We need to talk. I'm outside." Whilst walking fast towards the door she lets the girls know, "I have to pop out."

"Anywhere nice?"

"Just a bit of business, won't be long."

Pauline goes outside and Lee is sat in his car, clearly high and on edge. Pauline taps on window and makes him jump, Lee puts window down. "Quick, get in."

"What's up?"

"Just get in."

Pauline gets in and Lee looks at her wide-eyed and sweating.

"Look, if this is about earlier, I don't want to know."

"Earlier?"

"In there, Robert."

"No, no, it's fuck all to do with him, that's all laid to rest, so to speak. It's about Layla."

"Oh no, please don't tell me she's..."

"FUCK Polly, FUCK. What have I done?"

"I don't know, tell me."

"She's escaped."

"From where?"

"My mates place, left him for dead, that little bitch."

"Slow down Lee, I can't make sense of this. What are you telling me?"

"Polly, I had her bound up, coked up, trying to find out where the bag of coke is, three days I had her, she was about to break, only my mate passed out thinking he was fucking dying, she got away. I have to find her."

"Lee, the last place she would come would be to mine as we don't talk anymore, she did me over."

"If she goes to the Police."

"Trust me on that, she won't, she's not a snitch, she will be too scared."

"She better hadn't or I'll kill her, I was going to anyways but..."

"What? What for? That's too far Lee, she's not worth it."

"She knows something, I'm telling you, I could smell it. Now she's seen our faces."

"If she turns up here, which she won't, I will tell you, I promise. The police have been here asking but I've told them she's not working here anymore and I don't hear from her. How's your mate?"

"He's dandy, was just a panic attack. I can't go back inside Polly, I've got too many enemies."

"I'll keep my ear to the ground and ask about."

"Ok, I need to go, I'll drive around for a bit. I'll be in touch."

Pauline gets out of car and back into the Parlour. Sheila wants to go to the upstairs flat but nervous as does not know what she will find. Pauline comforts her and lets her know they will both be going in.

There are bottles, cans, cocaine remnants and broken ornaments on the floor, with some blood, not much - but looks like quite a bit of spatter.

Sheila's holds onto Pauline and both go quiet. Pauline turns to Sheila.

"No words needed, ever. Let's clean and pack any of his shit into a black bag and let this be the end of it."

Not even Pauline is fully aware of what has happened to Robert.

Both get busy and Pauline throws his stuff into his van and makes a call to 'fire-man Sam, out of ear shot from Sheila.

"White van outside mine, full of crap, take it somewhere, burn it. £150 Cash. Ask no questions. Keys are inside glove compartment. Thanks darling."

Pauline and Sheila walk back down into Parlour. A short while later, what looks like a punter, arrives bang on time for what is in diary. Pauline see's baseball cap, sunglasses and buzzes them in. The person takes their hat and shades come off to reveal themselves - it's Layla.

CHAPTER SEVEN

Pickles

"**Y**ou look like you've seen a ghost Polly."

"Bloody am by the looks of it. Look at the state of you."

"I know I've pissed you off, but I need your help."

"One good reason why I should put myself out for you?"

"It's about Lee."

"You best come in."

Layla and Pauline go into her bedroom and sit on the bed. Pauline makes it clear she does not want her here.

"Make it quick. I don't want the girls seeing you."

"Why?"

"You are bad news at the moment Layla, and everyone knows I'm not happy with you. Can't have people thinking I'm going soft. The police are looking for you, you're missing, all over the news. What have you got to say?"

"I haven't been missing on purpose, I was held hostage by Lee and his vile mate Darren."

"Whom you left for dead?"

"How the hell do you know that?"

"He's been here, looking for you."

"Darren?"

"No, Lee."

"Shit, please Polly, they were going to kill me. They are psychopaths and tripping out on all sorts of fucked up ideas about who did Gary over. They have got so many enemies, it's hard to break down who could have done it."

"Wish this would all just be done and dusted and wash away. I am pissed off with it all."

"I need to speak to the police."

"Don't grass on them Layla. They will destroy you if you do. Tell the police you have been having a break and just laid low for a while. They will need to physically see you to close a missing person file, so you'll have to go and see them."

"I will, maybe they have some info for me. I'll go in the morning, I need a wash and a sleep. I am exhausted."

"Do you know where the coke is?"

"Why is everyone asking me about this coke?"

"You lied to me, set up home around the corner and you've been off your head on the stuff, so does not take a genius."

"What are you talking about? Yes I have been doing coke but it's not connected to Gary, I know that much."

"Someone must know where it is. Lee is laser focused on finding it. Himself and Gary got it on tick, he knows he is trouble with the top guys if he does not recoup that loss."

"Lee said it was a big black bag full of it. Think I'd be sat here if I had huge amounts? I would have sold it and been travelling around Australia. You know that's my lifetime dream to travel around OZ if I had loads of money. I'd be gone, see ya later"

"So where did you get the money and afford to be shoving it up your nose?"

"A sugar daddy. I didn't want to tell you because I..."

"Get to the point."

"I met him here one day and he asked me to be solely his, in return for a flat and an allowance."

"You sneaky little cow. Who was he?"

"The one who turned up in the cowboy pants with his ass hanging out."

"He was a dish. He's rich?"

"Apparently, very rich. But he got bored of me, he didn't want to know after less than a week. I sat in that place waiting for him to come and see me a few days ago. He's married so could only see me occasionally, so when the doorbell went I assumed it was him and buzzed him in, but it was Lee and Darren, I had no idea who they were."

"Bloody hell, what a cobweb of fuck ups is this."

"As soon as Lee left Darren alone with me, he collapsed so I got out of there, sharp. I didn't care if he lived, he's mental."

"So you've not spoken to anyone else? You came straight here?"

"No I went to the flat cowboy got me but the locks have been changed and I looked in the window and it was empty, so I came here."

"You've been all over the news, the police have been here twice. Lee is hell-bent on finding you, the girls aren't happy with you - what the hell am I supposed to do with this?"

"Hand on my heart, I'm sorry, I know I messed up. I wanted out of this game and after the attack I rang cowboy and said yes to his offer. I thought the cowboy would be my way out, my chance to start over, no more sex for cash, just with him. I know it was wrong, but can you blame me? Being in that hospital bed shook me up."

"So you lost the baby?"

"What baby?"

"See, I knew you were lying, and that was even before the attack, so you've not been loyal."

"I must have been creeped out to say that, I was off my head, I can't recall. I was snorting that day too."

"I know, I saw you through the crack of the door."

"I've been numbing the pain with it, it helps."

"Not in the long run, it messes your head up, I should know, it did that to me. I know what it does and I know you screwed up, but it's not a case of going straight back to square one."

"And I don't expect it to. Just, I can't go to the Police and tell them, I now have nowhere to stay, I feel lost. Lee will do me more harm. I don't mind admitting I am petrified of them."

"I need to think long and hard. You need to lie low for a bit. My mate runs a small guest house up near the Seven Dials, stay there for a week, rest, keep out of the way and let it all the blow over. I told him it wasn't you but he won't leave no stone unturned until he gets that goddamn cocaine. Until it's found Lee won't stop hounding you, especially now you've run from him."

"Polly, I am so grateful. You really are the best. You've done more for me than anyone else in my life. I love you"

Pauline has never heard her be like this and thinks she's after money. "Don't tell me, you need some money. Here have this" Pauline goes to grab her purse.

"No I don't need it, honestly, it's fine."

Pauline stuffs £50 into her pocket anyway, and does not take no for an answer.

"Please, take it, just chill on your own for a bit, bubble baths, have a smoke, watch movies, just don't be about town. Your body needs to recover, properly."

"Pinky promise Polly. I will grab a cab on the way."

"It's Montpelier Guest house, right by the seven eleven store."

"Oh I know it, did a punter in there one night, it's gorgeous."

"Yes, so keep it nice. Karen is a bit anal about cleanliness, keep it tidy and she will respect you for it".

"I will, thank you so much. Thank you for everything."

Pauline feels she's being weird, a bit too kind, but brushes it off as related to recent trauma.

"I have a head full of crap to sift through. I will call in a couple of days ok."

"Deal."

Layla is fragile and half bent over but grabs Pauline's arm and pulls her inwards to her and hugs her. Even though she's looking like she has been in a bad accident she leaves as promptly as possible trying to look like she's fine. Layla looks back at Pauline. "We've had some fun here haven't we?"

"Plenty more to come too. When you're healed and better you can come back to work."

"Bye Polly." Layla walks off leaving Pauline worried about her, wondering if she will be ok.

The front door buzzes and Pauline can see its two new girls who have arrived for an interview to work upstairs.

Emma is 23, mousy shoulder-length scruffy hair, blue eyes, faux fur coat, little shiny shorts and boob tube, thick Bristolian accent and a spliff in hand and Julia, 30, Londoner, gym bunny, toned, cocky, full of herself.

"You must be Emma and Julia."

"Ten out of ten for observation skills darlin'." Julia trying to be cool.

"Want me to slam this door shut with you on the other side and start again or simply just fuck off? Your call."

"No, sorry I was just trying to be funny."

"Funny doesn't make money."

"Told you cocker, don't upset the Madame, ever."

"I know how it all works Emma. Pauline, I've been working with just Emma in my house in London for a few years. I'll have to get used to having a boss again."

"That's if I hire you."

"Yeah, sorry mate."

"I'm not your mate. Right come up to Polly's Parlour 2, show you around and we can have a chat."

"Cool, working in your new branch, sounds ace." Emma sort of slurs.

"Are you always stoned?" Pauline bluntly asks.

"I love the ganja, chills my hectic head out ya know?"

"Not when on shift, in front of my punters."

"Nah, no way hozzay. I have a little one before work, gets me into it and then one when I finish, to level me out. It's lush Pauline, want some?"

"No, I don't thank you. As long as we are clear - no drugs whilst on duty?"

"Told you it wouldn't be allowed Emma."

All three enter the upstairs apartment. Coming down the stairs towards them, on the communal hallway, is a gay man, Jake is mid 20s, brash and loud, with a fishnet crop top, white denim shorts, over sized sunglasses and love bites on his neck.

"Hey girls." His voice echoing throughout the hallway.

"Hello darling, not seen you around for a long time." Pauline gives him a little quick hug.

"I've been in away in Gran Canaria, working for a few months."

Emma beams with her own memory. "Bet that was a hoot. It's lush on that island, been twice, pure partying innit?"

"Just awesome. It's a beautiful atmosphere over there."

"Working the clubs and bars?" Asks Pauline.

"Part-time yeah. And part-time rent boy, made a killing sometimes."

"I didn't know you were on the game."

"Hell yeah, bugger working all the hours god sends, for peanuts, when there're richer nuts to make money from, if you know what I mean."

"We're going to be working in Polly's Parlour."

"MAY be working, I've not hired you yet."

'Sorry, yeah, may be." Says Emma.

"Well, if you do I'll see you around, just off to do an out call. Was nice to meet you. Polly, I'll pop down soon for a catch up?"

"I'd love that darling. See you later."

Jake leaves, all three enter the apartment.

"So, this is it. There're three bedrooms, one is occupied by Sheila. What hours are you wanting?"

"You said on the phone accommodation is possible too?"

"Yes, but not for free, it'll be taken out of your wages, but if you share a room, that'll bring the price down."

"Yeah, we will share. What's Sheila like?"

"She's one of my best. Young, but an absolute gem, she's chilled and you'll both adore her."

"Weed smoker then?"

"Nope, not everyone needs dope to relax Emma."

"Sweet, be nice to meet her." Julia sounding genuine.

Pauline shows them around and tells them how it'll be run.

"So, the calls will come in via downstairs and receptionist, Lisa, or I, will take bookings and we will let you know who's booked who and for what. For walk-ins off the street, you will need to let us know if anyone knocks this door. I need to know at ALL times who's here. Safety is paramount girls. Any areas you don't want to touch on?"

"Julia jumps in first. "Hell no, I am up for most, oh apart from girl on girl, that's one area I can't do."

Emma being open. "We've done it together before."

"That was one off. It repulsed me."

"Wow."

"Not you, just, you know, pussy, it's not my bag." Julia reassures Emma.

"Great Julia, thanks. Emma, any limits for you?"

"Not really love, no, oh hang on...." Her thick west country accent is cheering Pauline up, she loves it. "Definitely not anyone who's into ice cream, I can't cope with a cold fanny ever again."

"Sorry, what?"

"I thought a punter said 69er but turned up at the door with a 99er. So, yeah, he wanted to put it all down there, flake an all, then ate it. Swear to god Poll's, I swear I had frost bite on my Latvia."

"Don't you mean vulva?"

"Same thing innit my lover."

"No, Latvia is a country."

"Oh my god, all my life I've called it that."

"Lord give me strength!"

Pauline and Julia crack up laughing.

The sound of an ice cream van bellows in the distance, which makes all them howl with laughter even more. The tune is perfect timing.

Emma starts to run to the door, shouting;

"COME ON LADIES, LET'S GET A 99ER."

Emma opens door and trips over as an ice cream van slowly rolls past. Emma, through tears, screams;

"WAIT UP MR WHIPPY DRIVER. I NEED A 99ER. I NEED TO WORK THROUGH SOME PAST TRAUMA."

The van doesn't stop. Pauline, Julia and Emma are all keeled over on the doorstep. This is a gut crunching, laughing fit that keeps going. This is a memory they will always laugh at it - a bonding moment.

Pauline wipes her tears and tries to compose herself.

"Bloody hell girls, the best interview I've ever done."

"So, is that a yes?"

Pauline looks them both in the eyes and smiles. "Start tomorrow. Welcome to Polly's Parlour 2."

"Wow. You're mint Pauline. I love the vibe here." Emma's Bristol accent even stronger with each drag she takes.

"Let's hope you feel that when you're not so 'skunked up'."

"Trust me, I know a good heart when I meet one, ain't that right Jules? I got good gut instincts."

"You sure have. We won't let you down Pauline. I can't wait to start RTW."

"What's that? Sounds like a disease."

"R.T.W = Rinse the wallets. You know, milk the men for..."

"Yes, I get the picture." Pauline cuts in. "That's funny. I have a feeling you'll both enjoy it here. Where's your stuff?"

"In our little camper van, over the road." Emma points to it as they all walk out onto the path.

Pauline points out to a run down camper with tape on cracks of roof, rusty, with coloured flowers painted all over it. "You mean to tell me you've both been living in that?"

"Only for a week." Says Julia. "I lost my place due to rent arrears and we bumped into your mate who said calling you would put an end to our off grid camper life."

"Yes, Andy, he's a lovely guy, does the door here most nights. Sometimes it's just the most perfect timing; you were looking for work and a home and I need a job and home filled, win-win. Make yourselves at home and I will make a list of what's needed, towels etc."

Emma feels free enough to be honest already. "Don't you be worrying about all that Poll's."

"Less of the "Poll's.""

"Bollocks, so sorry."

"It's fine Emma, just, Pauline for now."

"OK, noted. What was I saying? Ah, yeah, we are top grade lifters, steal anything you need."

"No, no, no. No stolen shit at my door, everything to be above board. Understood?" Pauline reasserts herself and gains control, showing she's still the boss lady.

"Definitely Pauline." Emma commits. "Definitely won't go against the grain here."

"Yep, totally. What about for our own products, not business related?" Asks Julia.

"Such as?"

"Make up, tampax, knickers."

Pauline rolls her eyes as she's walking down the steps to her Parlour.

"Just, be careful. Security is tight in the stores around here. I will make a list and go with you to shops tomorrow to get what we need. Definitely no stealing when out with me. What you do after is your story, write what you like in it but don't pull me anywhere near where the law is involved when you are making your decisions in & out of my Parlour. I make sure they have extremely minimal traces of me on their radar. These lot are corrupt twats. Make sure you keep things tight. Right you two, down here after you've settled in, come meet the Pollettes!"

"Yes, what a cool name. See you shortly and Polls, shit, sorry, I mean, Pauline, thank you. Honestly, this touches my soul." Emma is high and it shows in her blood shot eyes.

"Very moving. Less smoke OK. Need to you to be present, not up in the clouds."

"I'm on it. I promise you, we will make you good money."

Emma & Julia walk over to their camper van, Pauline goes back into the downstairs Parlour.

Pauline is annoyed no one is at reception, the phone rings, reluctantly she answers it abruptly.

"YES?"

"How much for 10 minutes?"

"Ten grand, now fuck off."

Pauline slams phone down and storms through the lounge, and can see all her staff sitting out the back in the courtyard, smoking and laughing. Pauline dives in amongst the girls.

"This is a well established gentleman's, high class Parlour, not fuuuccckkking crufts. Sort your barnet's out, look presentable, get rid of the fag breath and get to work. Lisa, reception, girls laundry, wash dishes, come on, quick to it. I don't care who does what, just crack on."

All girls scatter, heads bowed as Pauline mutters she has a million things to do.

Later Pauline takes a call from Teddy, the slave, but forgot about the time - it's now 10pm.

"Good evening Polly, Teddy here. I did ring at 6, but no one answered."

"Oh Teddy I am so sorry I missed your call earlier, been rushed off of my feet. How are you, Mr Bundy?"

"Very witty dear. I was wondering if the receptionist has given it some thought?"

Pauline has been so occupied and Lisa has been busy, she hasn't had time to talk with Lisa.

"Yes, she is very up for it. I will tell Madame flatulence you need some variety, don't ever want to hurt her feelings."

"Did you speak to her about her gassy innards?"

Pauline hasn't spoken to her either, but knows she will speak to her and Lisa today, so kind of telling the truth.

"Yes, some issues with bran flakes I think she said, fibre reaction."

"I see. I would like to book Mistress as soon as possible."

"That's great Teddy, so that's brutal punishment, with Mistress..." Pauline tries to quickly think of a new title for Lisa's dominatrix role. "Mistress Marilyn. That will be as of next week if that suits?"

Teddy very enthusiastic about this and tells Pauline, "I simply cannot wait, I hope she leaves some great marks on my body. I want it full on."

She's never witnessed Lisa being anything other than smiling, bubbly and cute. Pauline believes in her and wants to throw her in at the deep end on this avenue, so she makes money and becomes more confident.

"She packs a punch, let me tell you. You will love it."

Teddy starts breathing heavily down the phone. "I shall dream of nothing but until then. Blessings to you Polly, see you soon. Thank you."

"My pleasure Teddy. See you then."

The following morning Pauline started her day with a brunch picnic in a park, with Matthew laying out croissants, strawberries, champagne and giving her lingering kisses. Matthew is giving affection like she's never had and its making her feel beautiful. Planning a trip away before telling all the girls she will be taking time off, feels like a bonding time for them both. Matthew and Pauline are going to take a month out from life and spend it together. Both are excited at their plans to get away and see what develops between them.

Lisa has another appointment with Colin at his parents' old run down farm. Her last few appointments have been at night, when Colin's parents have been asleep. However, today, it's a day visit, as they are off out for the day, and Colin has it all set up in one of the old barns. Lisa has been informed it will be a surprise and that she will love it. In her other visits she's been a pig, a goat and a sheep dog, which she found a bit creepy, but is clinging onto her conversations with Pauline about being strong and making money. Just knowing she HAS to do it to pay the dealers off for her mum, is fighting an inner conflict. She has chosen when to hop down from her reception chair and work in the bedroom, having to do this to pay it all to someone else hasn't put her in the best of moods in the taxi.

"Can you turn the radio up please? I love this song."

Driver turns it up and blares out 'Genie in a bottle'. Lisa winds the window down and lets the sun on her face and the air blow through her hair as she puts her head out of the window, singing.

When she arrives, Lisa walks down to the barn, as instructed. There is no noise and no sign of any people and starts thinking she has the wrong day, worried she may bump into his parents. An old barn door creeks as she slides it open and sees a bag with a note for her. Inside the bag is a very expensive donkey outfit. The note reads;

Dear Little Donkey, a.k.a Pickles,

Please can you trot down to the adjoining field when you are ready. Please do not speak but please feel free to make 'eee-oorrr' noises as you approach the gate. Look forward to riding you.

Colin. X

Lisa's heart sinks and the thought of him on her back has made her sit on an old barrel and ponder if this humiliating has gone too far. The outfit gets put on half-heartedly and keeps telling herself one day she will look back on this and laugh. For now, she makes her way, a slight hopping rather than trotting and trying to see where she's going without falling. Up ahead she sees Colin through the eye slits and starts to make donkey noises, but sounds more like a seagull in pain.

"Whoahhhh, hello pickles, steady up there little donkey, who's a good girl."

"Hi Colin."

"What did the instructions say.....DON'T speak."

Colin takes a crop from the side of his green wellington boot and canes pickles bottom.

"Bad Pickles. Bad girl."

The padding on the outfit means Lisa barely feels it. Colin is whipping like he's on a race horse near the finish line, battering the behind and shouting. "Bad bad girl. Now get in the paddock." Colin pushes her in through the gate and he ties her up to the fence. Colin rams a carrot into the mouth slot and puts a saddle on her and hops on her. Lisa takes two steps and collapses under the weight. Colin hurts his hip and yelps in pain.

Lisa takes the head piece off and speak to him. "I am so sorry. I broke my back years ago and two of my discs are ruined. I won't be able to do this."

Colin starts to cry and opens up to Lisa.
"This is the reason why I still live at home with my parents. I am weird, not right in the head, I deserve to be in trouble."

"Why? What's wrong?"

"My parents had animals and just me, no other kids, just me here playing on my own. When I hit my teens I was socially awkward and had no mates, so the animals became my friends. But my mum caught me fingering a ferret, then my dad caught me inside of a cow. They knew I was lonely and exploring but threatened to sell all the animals."

Looking around at empty fields. "I am guessing they did then."

"Not straight away. I was really well-behaved and one day my Dad brought home a donkey, Pickles, and it looked at me in a funny way. I don't know how to put this feeling into words, but it was like Pickles wanted me, fancied me, kept staring at me."

"Right, ok." Lisa starts getting freaked out by this admission. "So what was your next move?"

"I had a wet dream I got Pickles pregnant and the dream was occupying my mind, day and night. The urge to fist her got so strong that I sneaked out in the night and brought her into the stables and put a blanket down. Within minutes I was elbow deep and she was letting out a roar which sounded like she was loving it but my parents ran down and caught me, red, well brown, handed."

"Oh wow. What did they say?"

"My mum cried, my Dad was more interested if I had cut my nails as I played guitar and had a long thumb nail, so naturally he was worried if I'd made a tear inside of Pickles, but she was fine. They sold almost all of our animals and told me never to leave home because I would be hated and made fun of for my animal obsession."

"I see." Lisa has no idea how to respond to this and is feeling uncomfortable, and foolish, dressed as half a donkey.

Colin comes up with an idea and shares it. "Can you put the head back and rain on me."

"Excuse me?" Lisa knows exactly what he means.

"You know, crouch over me and piss...."

"No, no way. That's not..." Lisa thinks of the money. This is the last session before she has to pay off the crooks, so breathes deep and wants to give in. "I can't, I've got loose bowels, and I had a curry last night, so best not." Lisa feels sure she can go now.

"That's even better. Let's do it."

"No, Colin, NO. That is NOT happening."

"I am so sorry, I am trying to get a healthy balance and keep screwing it up."

"You mean you've done this before?"

"Years ago, but I put her off."

"Why?"

"I put a rod through the back of her dress then put her on top of a roasting tray, put a pig mask on her and started spinning her like she was hog roast, but she fell off and broke her neck. I had no choice but to call an ambulance. They came here, sirens blaring and waking my parents up. They came to the barn and seen the set up and I was threatened with them telling the police, and I would lose my job. The young lady did not want anyone knowing she was a prostitute, so I got away with that one. From then on my feelings have been dormant."

"Wow. May I ask why you do it?"

"It's the thrill of going against what my parents want, what they expect. Don't knock it until you try it."

""Col, no offence, but it's a bit too 'out there' for me."

Colin was about to get defensive but the sound of his mum, Beryl, shouting across the land, "Darling we are home. Colin, where are you!" brings him to a halt.

Lisa looks into his eyes and wonders what the hell goes on at this farm. "Colin what shall I do?"

Beryl, has made it to the gate. Lisa gets up and has her tits out up top, the donkey face under her arm and wearing the bottom donkey outfit. Beryl freezes on the spot, Colin stays sat in fear. Lisa smiles sweetly and makes her way over to Beryl, Colin follows with bowed head. Lisa whispers through her teeth, like a professional ventriloquist. "Back me up, trust me."

Colin is regretting his whole life at this moment, Beryl looks steaming. Lisa opens up the conversation with an over the top greeting, for a reason she doesn't even know, most likely through nerves, puts on a Russian accent.

"Hello, how lovely to meet you. I'm Valderine Mishkov." Lisa is thrilled she can be so thoughtful in times of crisis.

Beryl gives a suspicious smile and speaks fluent Russian, for what seems like an hour. Lisa looks on and has no idea how to get out of this and is shaking. Beryl then speaks in English and asks her why she did not speak back in Russian. Lisa explains, in her new accent - "I come here for a better life as a little orphan, so my Russian was not needed."

"And what are you doing here on my land?"

"I am a healer and spiritual advisor. I have been seeing your son for months and we have come to an end now. He is no longer into animals, the desires are crushed. I put this on to see the levels of temptation and he didn't engage in anything other than positive conversations. Congratulations, you've got your son back."

Beryl's creases in her forehead become more apparent the more she tries to work this out and get a sense of its truth. Beryl likes the look of Lisa's face and wonders if there could be anything between her and Colin. Colin is dying inside, whilst Beryl makes more hints. Lisa makes her excuses and says she has a cab ordered, picking her up at the farm entrance any minute. Lisa gives them both a peck on the cheek and walks away to get changed and leaves. When she looks back she sees Colin hugging his mum, she feels she really did some healing, even if it was not authentic, it still worked.

Back at the Parlour, Jake visits. Lisa lets him in and shows him through to the back yard to join Pauline, who's sipping tea and smoking, with her face pointed up to the sun.

"Hey girl. Getting roasted? You need to put sun cream on that old leather face."

"Says the sun-bed queen."

"Touché."

"Are you alright? Didn't want to say it in front of the girls but I can see sadness in your eyes."

"If I let myself cry, it'll be like a tsunami, I can't let that happen, not yet."

"Oh Darling, why?"

"I am so skint and feel low, dunno why. I spent loads of money on partying in Gran Canaria, and loved the busy life there but I was robbed of all my jewellery and what cash I had left and the fella I was seeing split with me as he found out I was on the game over there. I've set a trail of destruction, which I need to clear up, but I'm stuck. I just put cards out to get some work. It's tough competition around here. I'm not making much, men want it as cheap as possible, always wanting longer for free or haggling on the phone. When I started there were about 4 rent boys advertising in the newsagent window, now the whole window is chock-a-block. I just went in there with a mate and we told the owner we would tidy it up for him. So we threw a few away, made it look neat and put our cards slap bang in the middle with fluorescent pens highlighting our cards."

"That's hilarious Jake, I like your style. As you're good at advertising, I could do with someone like you putting some cards out for the girls, at 20 quid a round, and a few hours on reception to give Lisa a break, and some odd jobs, if you're up for it? Be perfect with you living upstairs."

Pauline hasn't known Jake on a deep level, it's been more in passing and little chats here and there, so feels proud she's trusting to have someone relatively new in her Parlour working. Therapy has been a much-needed addition to her life, as if it came at the right time. Trusting Matthew has been the biggest shift for her. With him she feels a balance, not being submissive and under someone's thumb, but an equal and healthy feeling.

Jake is over the moon at this and shows her he's eager.

"This is perfect timing as I need every penny as I want to save and get out of here in the next couple of years. My head feels fried from all the partying and drugs, so I will say yes to that most definitely. Cheers. When can I start?"

"Start tonight 7 o'clock, first round, second round at 10pm. Cover Lisa on reception when she next wants some time off."

"Ahh, I'm busy tonight."

Pauline slips back into business woman mode and lets it be known that the Parlour has to be his commitment or walk.

"No worries, someone I know is desperate for a job, so..."

"No, no, it's just that I have a punter booked in and..."

"You either want it or you don't."

"I do, honestly. I will cancel him."

"Tell him you need to reschedule, don't say cancel, they hate that word, it's too rejecting to them."

"Christ, yeah, I didn't think about that."

"Jake, you learn a lot over the years in this business. I will get

Lisa to help you get to grips with how reception is run and start putting the girls' cards out into the telephone boxes."

"Sure, thanks. This will sort my head out, and keep me focused. Highlight any errors I make as I learn quickly in anything I do. I won't let you down."

"Don't worry about that kiddo, I've got eyes on every detail of this place. I will have you working like a machine by the end of your apprenticeship here."

This tickles Jake, he's ready for change and this could be it; away from drugs, single lane, some work which can lead to more hours and personal punters himself - this is a good day.

Noises upstairs in the form of loud pop music, seems a bit too loud and irritates Pauline whilst she's speaking to Jake.
"I will be putting a stop to that in a sec."
Pauline points up to ceiling.
"I will see you later Jake, welcome to Polly's Parlour." She extends her hand.

Jake is chuffed to bits and shakes her hand tightly.

"Yes, the best news all year. I take it they are joining the team." Jake also points to ceiling. "They seem like fun."

"So far so sweet, yes, a good vibe from them. I'm going up, let's drop in on them."

Pauline takes Jake and lets them in with her keys. The new girls are prancing around the lounge listening to the radio and drinking wine. Pauline and Jake look at each other and laughter strikes, as they see the girls on the sofa miming into a vibrator singing Madonna's 'like a virgin.'

Pauline waits for the song to end and lets them finish, she enjoys seeing them happy.

"Didn't take you long to settle in. I need you to come down and meet the rest of the girls. Nice toy by the way. Anne Summers?"

"Nah, from Soho. I've got a massive one of these too. This is just a handbag size so I can do myself when..."

"Right, I get the idea. Let's go down." Pauline leads the way.

Jake blows them a kiss and says he will be down in a bit. Departing with - "Fab to meet you ladies." Emma puts the vibrator in her pocket and follows Pauline, along with Julia.

As they are making their way down to Polly's Parlour, a car horn grabs Pauline's attention, she looks over to see a blue and white camper van pulling up. Pauline tells the girls to go on down to the Parlour, as she's struts over. Matthew is beaming with pride behind the wheel and Pauline's face lights up.

"I love this."

"Your carriage awaits, my lady. I cannot wait to take you away in this."

"This is so sweet of you. How much was it?"

"Ah not a lot, I can afford it."

"I need to drop this in for Maddie too whilst I am here." Matthew points to the back to show Pauline a metal contraption.

"What the hell is that?"

"Some equipment Maddie wanted."

Pauline heads back into the Parlour, with Matthew clanking on behind her with Maddie's metal. Pauline ushers him into office/ bedroom and walks into lounge, where Lisa, Maddie, Sheila, Julia, Emma & Leigh are all sat down and chatting.

"Where's Sandra?"

In the background they hear Sandra yelling with her punter. "Ah, yeah, baby, yes, first class, signed for. Your package has been rammed through my letterbox."

Pauline looks at the girls. "Postman popped in?"

"He's posted her parcel alright." Maddie's comment spreading, making all the girls laugh together.

Pauline composes herself. And turns to Maddie. "Your father is putting something together for you in the bedroom."

"Ace. About time."

"What is it?"

"I'll show you later. You'll love it"

"Look forward to it." Pauline sits in an arm chair and means business.

"Right, I was going to introduce you all to Julia and Emma, but see you're already acquainted. Rota - I want you all to sit together and sort out the shifts fairly, no bloody bickering or I will take back control of it. I am giving you a chance to be more business like, some responsibility so we feel like a collective, a team. You girls can be a lovely sisterhood, hold each other up when the chips are down, create some special memories. Sharing this side your life, in your prime, is something we will all look back on. I want you to look back with fondness and spine tingling memories of happiness and, most of all, success. The future is where the money needs to be thought of, not today, save money so you can be independent later on. You might crack a hip or two on this job and I don't pay compensation, your contract states this is all on your shoulders, so be wise with the dirty dollars! Just work as many hours as you can."

Pauline is in Momma mode and this always captures the room when she is in a caring mood and the girls love it.

"I need to take a bit of a back seat, spend some time with Matthew and hand a little responsibility over to you Lisa. I need a holiday, some weekends off and enjoy myself a bit more. Being with Matthew soothes my anxiety. My heart doesn't pound with panic when I am out of town and with him. Being in this Parlour is magical to me, it will always be home. I just need to show Matthew I appreciate him, share some of my life with him." Pauline's eyes have glazed over and looks smitten in her sparkling eyes.

"Pardon Polly? Me?" Lisa only heard her name more than anything else in Pauline's speech.

"That's correct. Jake is going to put in some hours on reception and card runs so you get a break. l need someone to hold fort when I am off, you're my chosen one. Few extra bucks for you obviously, plus you have some farm animal fun to do."

"Oh yeah, how's that gig going?" Sheila asks.

"I was there yesterday as a donkey, long story. He pays great money but it all got a bit weird for me"

Sandra lets her postman punter out, then back into the lounge, with a postage stamp stuck to her chin without realising.

"I see you went down to head office." Leigh jokes.

"Eh?"

Pauline points to her chin so Sandra feels her chin and the stamp comes off in her hand. "Oh my God."

"What's up?"

"It's second bloody class."

"Be thankful it's not a returns label." Maddie jokes.

Sandra has her back up, out of nowhere. "What the fuck is that supposed to mean? Just because you're trapped in that chair doesn't mean I won't swing for you."

"Who the fuck are you talking to? I am princess paraplegic remember. Swing for me old lady, and I'll ruin your toes with these wheels."

Sandra didn't expect Maddie to be this feisty, so responds calmly. "I'm just not in the mood today Maddie."

"Nor am I. So settle yourself, it's yawn."

Pauline has heard enough. "Right, you two, grow up. I will not have friction in here, it spoils the ambience. Sort your crap out and come together, we are a team."

Sandra and Maddie shake hands, but it looks and feels insincere. Outside Pauline has been chatting with Mathew for a while, in the back yard. He took far too long putting together Maddie's contraption in the bedroom. They are chatting over a glass of wine and talk about their up coming trip.

When Matthew leaves he gives her a long lingering kiss, Pauline almost melts when they kiss and pats him hard on the ass.

Pauline walks into Maddie's room and sees her hanging in mid-air in a hoist like you would see in a hospital or nursing home. Maddie has the remote control and is moving the left to right buttons, meaning it's swinging her around.

"What the fuck is this all about?"

"Today I am a Wimbledon ball girl and my next man is gonna come in as a professional tennis player and his first strike is to knock me out with the tennis ball to my head and then I am just limp, just hanging for him to do whatever he needs to do next, which I'm not sure what he will do yet."

"Love 15 darling, well done."

The door buzzer goes, Pauline looks on the intercom and sees an older man with a little white shorts, tennis racket and ball, with a white cap.

"Hello Derek, I have not seen you for a while. This is a new concept?"

"Just some failed career moments I experienced, which I need to explore."

"You go careful with those big balls."

"Don't you worry about that Polly, I will be gentle-ish."

"Right, well, go on through, she's on centre court. Go play your match."

Derek becomes sweaty and salivation at the lips. "Don't suppose you've got a punnet of strawberries?"

"Don't push your luck."

"Sorry, I was just joking. Thank you, see you shortly."

Derek skips off to 'centre court', whilst Pauline walks up to her next counselling session looking forward to it.

Pauline's heart skips a beat when she turns a corner and see's Jake sitting outside a coffee shop, with Belinda.

Pauline stands in the doorway of a clothes shop opposite, and watches for a couple of minutes. With blood boiling, she decides not to act on it and deal with it later or she will be late for her appointment.

CHAPTER EIGHT

Daddy Issues

By the time she gets to the therapy room Pauline has calmed down and can't wait to show Terry what she has written.

"Hey Terry. I did what you asked, I wrote something."

Terry is pleased and sits down to listen as Pauline decides to stand up for this, and reads it out loud.

"Poem, written by Pauline Cochran," she declares. Pauline clears her throat and proceeds...

Once a lost child, screaming out for attention,

As if I had something to say.

But when confronted I would close down,

I only felt safe enough to speak when I'd pray.

Asking whoever was listening - why I was being punished,

For feeling natural in my own skin.

But for others to look on in disgust,

No matter how far I would run, I couldn't win.

Nobody liked the boy in his mum's wedding dress,
Nor play with him in his football kit.
It seemed as though I was running my own show,
Like I was the only one who gave a shit.

He was a chunk of my past I am fond of,
He was a part of me biologically.
For every other part of my life he was like a stranger,
So far removed from who I was mentally.

My spiritual path, my authentic self & heart,
Shone brighter when I departed from him aesthetically.
The mirror was no longer a dark place to stand,
I finally saw a reflection that made sense to me.

I have found myself when I went out on my own,
And believe I've found happiness.
My mothers death only leaves my father,
He can choke to death on his bitterness.

Terry is a little taken back by the last line, but congratulates her firstly on a poem so raw and honest.

"Pauline that's very reflective and shows real truth."

Pauline is grinning, loving that she's impressed a therapist with words. "Aw cheers Terry."

"That last line packs a punch."

"Yeah well." Pauline shrugs her shoulders. "Fuck him. Not seen him for 34 years, wouldn't even know him if I passed him in the street. Last I heard he was in London. I am glad I never bumped into him when I lived there. I feel like everything is aligned and in place for me."

Terry looks on fondly and discusses with Pauline her new relationship, trip away and so much in this session that she leaves feeling drained and thinking loads about her father.

As she passes the cafe she sees Jake still sat there, but on his own eating lunch. Pauline approaches without him seeing and sits down next to him.

"Alright Jake, looking a bit lonely here on your own."

"Hey love, where did you spring from?"

"Just walking back to mine. I saw you here earlier." Pauline gives him an opportunity to bring up Belinda.

Jake eats a mouthful of his cheesy chips. "Mmm these are the best. Help yourself." No mention of Belinda as he pushes the bowl towards Pauline.

"No thanks." Pauline feels her blood boil but is trying to put the calmness she's learned in therapy into good use. Deep breath, usually works.

"How long you been sat here?"

Jake is none the wiser to the shift in her demeanour. "Hour and a half-ish. Why?"

Pauline feels she's given him a chance. "You can fuck off if you think you're working for me."

Jake is in utter shock and genuinely no idea why she's acting aggressive. "Errmm what the fuck has got into you?"

"Belinda, that's why?" Don't deny you know her, seen you sat here earlier - laughing away." Pauline mimics a fake laugh to take the piss.

"The drag queen?"

"Looks like one, granted, but transvestite is the word you need."

"I don't know her. She sat down and started chatting, she's funny."

"Funny to look at, that's about it."

"What's the story between you two? In conversation she asked where I work and when I said Polly's Parlour, the reaction was a bit strange."

"In what way?"

"Like she was upset then asked how we get on. When I said we've known each other for a while I felt, umm, not sure how to describe it...like she cares for you a lot."

"She's dark, be careful of her"

"What happened?"

"Can't be arsed to go into it, water under the collapsed bridge. No going back. She's untrustworthy, did me a bad deal. Don't ever tell her anything about me ever again."

"Of course, chill, no problem."

Pauline doesn't appreciate the chill comment. "I will chill *you* if you're not careful...into the local morgue fridge."

Jake loves this and cracks up laughing. Pauline holds it in and gives the evil eyes, this makes Jake laugh more and Pauline can't hold it and bursts out with him. Slight relief Jake does not know Belinda.

It's been a week, Lisa has hit the deadline and worked her magic to save 3.5K, so isn't worried she will only owe £500. Lisa was going to ask Pauline, but she feels Pauline has done more than enough for her, and sure the thugs will be cool with this, so sets off, naively, to her mother's house.

When Lisa enters its silent, she feels on edge, quietly closes the door behind her and walks on her toes towards the lounge. The door is open a jar, Lisa pushes it slowly and see's her mum on the sofa curled up, she looks dead. Lisa strides to the sofa and kneels down to hold her mum. A mutter of "Hello love" lets Lisa know she's alive. Lisa lets out a huge sigh of relief. Mum, Maureen, sits up and seems fresh but withdrawn. "I thought you were gone, nearly gave me a heart attack mum. I have been worried sick about you all week."

"Why would you be worried? I am fine honey."

"You weren't this time last week."

"What do you mean?"

"You don't remember? I am here to pay off a huge debt, with interest on your behalf or you'll be dead."

Laughing at Lisa. "You've been watching too many films."

"Mum, there were two men here last week, you had a needle hanging out of your arm and I agreed to pay your drug debt."

Maureen's mood changes, looks around the room. "Why can't I remember much these days?"

Lisa notices she is different. Maureen has always been functioning and does well when not on drugs, today is unusual. Lisa can tell she has not had heroin, but she's slow and seems confused.

"Mum, have you taken something today?"

"No, not had anything. I woke up on the sofa yesterday and made myself take a shower, and today. I had a Valium yesterday but I am out of everything today. Can you get me some babe, I'll pay you back."

"You can piss off. I am paying men today to keep you alive, can you grasp that? To keep you ALIVE, for fuck's sake. And you want me to lend you money to inject shit into your veins. I may as well keep the money and let them finish you off."

"Don't be like that." Maureen tilts her head and looks at Lisa with sadness. "I am getting clean."

"It's like you're on loop mum, same words, different week, that's all. I have had to work so hard for this money."

Lisa hasn't noticed the men are at the patio glass door and sliding it open quietly.

"I have made three and half grand at Polly's Parlour and it's still not enough."

Maureen's eyes widen as she looks over Lisa's shoulder. Lisa can feel them behind her.

"Did I just hear you don't have all the money?" Says the tallest one of the two, and the only one who talks. The other one seems to be on mute again, but both in balaclavas.

Lisa spins round and stands up. "I'm only 500 short, but I can get that in a few days, I swear I can."

"Now where can a girl earn this amount of money? Polly's Parlour we hear you say, I know that place. Interesting. Now we know you're a whore, maybe you can work it off? Both of us at the same time?"

"I am just the receptionist. I get good tips that's all. This was my savings too."

"Ask your mother if she wants to die."

"What, wait, no look - I've got cash, three thousand five hundred."

"We said 4." He looks at Lisa and Maureen's hands and grabs Maureen's left hand and starts to take her two rings off, from her wedding finger.

"No please don't, that all she has left of my Dad, have mine."

He takes Maureen's rings then grabs Lisa's hand and rubs his fingers smoothly over her rings and hand, looking at her, smiling oddly.

"Not much profit on Argos jewellery love, I have an idea though."

Lisa perks up thinking he is going to be soft and either let her off or do a deal which works for both of them.

"OK, What is it?"

"How about we fuck your mum to work off the money?"

"No, please."

Maureen is stone-cold silent with fear, she has no idea what's going on and takes Lisa's hand and gets her to sit down next to her.

"Lisa I can't, you know I've got a colostomy bag."

"What, since when?"

"Ladies, ladies, shut it. You, up." Pointing to Maureen.

Maureen starts to shake and hunches her shoulders over and bows her head as she gets up and walks towards him. Lisa starts to well up, and pleads with the men.

"I am begging you, please don't hurt her."

"No other way, unless you want this." He grabs his crotch and rubs it. "Prime British beef baby."

"No, never, nor my mum."

Lisa stands up and puts her hand out to her mum. Maureen slightly moves forward and he grips her wrist tight and makes her kiss him, pulling her hard to his face. Maureen doesn't move her lips, so he slobbers all over her mouth and snogs her and licks her tense lips, whilst rubbing her crotch at the same time. Maureen has grey leggings on, so Lisa can see the effort he is putting in to push his hand hard into the creases. Lisa is in shock, and tries one last time to ease this situation.

"I can get the money, please, day after tomorrow, I am begging you."

With a gun in his hand, he points it at Lisa. "How would you be able to raise that in 24 hours?"

"I am not working tomorrow, but the day after I am and I will borrow it from the cash tin at work. I can borrow 500 easily." Lisa is in panic mode, does not know what to say. She will say anything to see them let go of her mum, this has to work.

"Now - or she gets it." He puts the gun to Maureen's forehead.

Lisa cries, standing alone looking at the floor, knowing they are like a pack of animals, about to ruin her mum. Lisa has the gun pointed at her, so sits down and sobs into her hands, not wanting to look.

Lisa is ordered to look up, but won't, she does not want to see this vision of horror. The main man pulls her by the hair and makes her look. Maureen is being taken from behind and fast, by his quiet sidekick. Maureen is trying to scream but a hand over her mouth prevents her. The roar is spine-chilling, the energy from these two men feels dark and brutal. Lisa will never un-see this, she glances to the side but can see the rape in her peripheral, so closes her eyes. He pulls her eyes open and makes her look for a minute. Lisa knows a moment like this is going to finish her mum off and demolish her mind after witnessing this. When he finishes Maureen is pushed down on the floor. "Debt cleared, nice one Maureen."

Lisa falls to the floor and cradles her mum as the two thugs fist bump each-other, laughing uncontrollably. "She's pretty tight for an old bird." They leave out of the front door, slamming it behind them.

Maureen has gone into shock and trembling. Lisa pulls her leggings and underwear up for her and gets her to sit up. Sweet tea with a valium is given to Maureen and slowly she comes around but falls asleep. Lisa lays next to her, staring at her face, close up, studying her lines, her shape, and sobs. This is the last place Lisa has any strength left to help her mum, it's been a lifetime of heartbreak and she's had the maximum amount of stress a human can take. It's time for one last shot; to get professional help. This means money and she knows exactly how to make it quickly.

The next day Lisa is looking drained and tired and was going to spend the day with her mum, but Jake has rang in sick, so goes into work. Lisa rings her grandmother and convinces her to let her mum go stay for a while to dry out, even though its failed numerous times, but cannot bear the thought of leaving her on her own. Pauline takes one look at Lisa when she arrives and knows her well enough to know something is wrong.

"Alright Lisa?"

Lisa smiles half-heartedly, looks down at diary and gives no eye contact. "All dandy thanks."

"Right, head up, look at me."

Lisa looks up with blood shot eyes. "Polly, I am so tired, stayed up until late watching movies."

"What did you watch?"

Lisa's head goes blank, she can't pull a name out. "Um, it was that new one."

"Called?"

"Oh, lord, what was it."

"Cut the crap, I know you, what's up?"

"Honestly, it's nothing."

"I know when something is wrong because there's always empty chocolate wrappers in the bin."

Pauline points to the bin, at least two family size chocolate wrappers showing.

"I don't want to talk about it."

"We always share stuff, you've got me worried. Something happened at the farm?"

"No, no, it's just."

Lisa stares at Pauline, the memory has pushed that fear onto her facial expression; pupils expanding, nervous twitch near her eye. "I paid those men but I was short so one of them forced himself on my mum, in front of me."

"What the fuck...oh darling, come here."

Pauline puts her arms out and Lisa walks into her welcoming embrace and cries her heart out.

"Oh Lisa, let it out, come on, bless your heart."

When Lisa leans out of Pauline's arms, she hold Pauline's hands and tells her what happened. Pauline is pissed off she did not ask her for the remainder of the money and that pride has no place when it comes to safety, but does not want to kick her whilst she is down.

"You call the police?"

"No, they won't do bugger all."

"Your poor mum. Where is she?"

"She's gone to my grandmothers for a few weeks, to relax and get off the gear, cold turkey. Last night has shook her, and me."

"You need some time off?"

Lisa likes to impress Pauline and follows her lead often, so refuses time out.

"No, we pick ourselves up and we get on with it, don't we?"

"Fair point, but the offer is there. That must have been horrendous to witness. Those mother fuckers. If at any time you need money Lisa, you must ask me, please don't deal with heavy stuff like that again. You know where the cash stash is, do not put yourself in danger ever again."

"Sorry, thank you. I will be ok. I'll get my head into my work."

"Talking about it might help. I will leave you my therapists number. If it gets too much call him OK?"

"Will do, I might just do that."

Pauline's mobile phone rings and she walks off to back yard with it.

Lisa has done farm animals all week, plus reception, sold load of things and been through the trauma of seeing it all happen to her mum. She has feelings of resentment for working to get all that money, to only now be without any money and have nothing to show for it, plus fighting with herself and inner demons to try and forget the money loss and focus on recovery for her mum and praying her mum does not get into this pit again. She would not be able to dig her out again, so plans in her head to get some money for rehab are now the driving force for living.

Sitting on her swivel chair she is sorting the diary and see's it's her and Sheila that are on shift, whilst upstairs Emma & Julia are covering.

Lisa has got into the sex side of things, because she's had no choice. Now she can see how much she can earn, she loves money even more. Letting that 3.5k go is killing her silently inside, but a sense of pride she has saved her mum, again.

The Phone rings with a unique request. Lisa is not her usual self but remains upbeat for the phone.
"Good morning, Polly's Parlour. How can I help you today?"

Man on the phone speaks eloquently to her. "Good morning to you too. I have seen on the web page there is a disabled girl working there and her speciality is blow jobs and she has a hoist?"

Lisa knows Maddie is off today, her thoughts go wild, she knows Maddie gets higher rates for special appointments, so in the moment she makes a decision because of what money makes her feel like; it's a buzz.
"Ah, it's your lucky day - that'll be me, I am on today."

"Fantastic. I need a tarty school girl, brunette hair, that I can put into the hoist."
Lisa is feeling a panic emotion but rolls with it, she needs this money.
He continues."I will stand naked and you push the button back and forward so you are kind of putting your whole body into the blow job, does that make sense?"

"Makes perfect sense."

Lisa does not like dicks in her mouth, so the fear of being sick has set in immediately, but plays along.

"I want to climax all over you, and the hoist, my heavy load almost blinding you and watch you 'stuck', begging to be released, but I take the control and wank myself off at your panic and disability and press all the buttons so you are mid-air, being swung in all directions. I will pay extra for the humiliation, obviously."

"Sounds ideal to me, that'll be £400." Her one shot at a nice sum, so worth a try."

"I beg your pardon."

"May sound extreme, but I am worth it. I am at the top of my game and the disability, cost of equipment, paying my carer, it all adds up. This is niche, I am worth every penny."

"I want 1.5 hours and I will give you £250."

Although her heart sinks, that's still great money.
"Deal. As long as you bring me sweets, chocolate and a bottle of Lucozade please."

"I think we got ourselves a deal. See you in an hour?"

Lisa tries to hide her excitement. "Perfect. See you soon, ermm, sorry I didn't catch your name."

"Henry."

"Ok, great Henry, see you soon."

Lisa gets straight down to business. She has a wash, thinks through a plan, dashing around, sorting Maddie's room for herself, and dresses up as a schoolgirl in a mini grey skirt, white shirt, tie, cakes the make up on and an auburn long wig. Henry wants 'tarty' so she's giving him full face, over the top, fake freckles, thicker lips and glasses. The wig is such a contrast from her blonde hair, which is in bunches with bows, she looks unrecognisable.

Lisa trying to be low-key but Pauline comes out of her bedroom and sees the back of Lisa going into Maddie's room, no longer called the office because Maddie has put a spice girls poster on the door and written "Maddie D's Room" on it. Pauline uses the loo then goes into Maddie's room. Lisa is adjusting the hoist and unaware Pauline has entered.

"Lisa, care to explain?"

Lisa jumps and faces Pauline. Lisa has always had massive respect for Pauline and never lies to her. Her immediate thought is to make something up on the spot, but opens up to Pauline. Lisa goes red in the face.

"Polly, I may have gotten myself into a bit of bother."

"I'm all ears."

Lisa squirms a little."I've said I have a disability to a punter on the phone and pretended to be Maddie."

Not quite the reaction Lisa was expecting, but Pauline laughs loudly. "You did whhaaat?"

"Good money though, and I need it after paying those wankers off, don't I?"

"So, what's your plan?"

"I was not going to tell anyone as I know it's quiet, hoping I could do this and get it over with, without Maddie finding out. I am so sorry Polly."

"I don't know why this is funny to me. So let's get this straight - you are pretending to be a disabled schoolgirl in a wheelchair?"

With a grin, mainly at the amusement of Pauline loving it, she continues.

"I will be the in the wheelchair when he arrives and he will undress me and transfer my limp body into the hoist for some sexual activity. He sounds really posh."

"You do realise that's a kids hoist? Maddie is 4ft 9 and slim. You're a 5ft 8 buxom blonde."

"It'll be fine, this is a sturdy one."

"Right, and who was going to answer the door exactly?"

"I was going to tell Sheila in a sec and get her to open door and see him through to me. His first sighting of me will be in Maddie's spare chair, thank God she keeps that here. I'll have to do something with my legs, so they look more....car crash victim-ish."

Pauline pulls a couple of small portions of hair off of Lisa's face and tucks it behind Lisa's ear. "I love how you think outside the box in times of need. Shows great business potential. Getting off reception now and then isn't so bad is it?"

"To be honest, I think I like it. Obviously the money is more and it's all safe fun."

"You've done well darling, keep it up, literally, and see how you go."

Lisa thinks big and forgets herself. In a ditsy manner, with eyes wide; "I could work my way to the top, open my own Parlour one day - 'Lisa's lush....'"

"Let me stop you there young lady, rewind, your OWN Parlour?"

"That came out wrong. I mean, one day, when you want to retire, I could take over or help run it."

"This old bird ain't retiring, ever."

"Good. You've been my rock the last couple years, I will be forever grateful for your kindness."

"My pleasure darling, you have been consistently loyal and hard-working. Now, let's get you ready to be disabled."

Lisa giggles. "Don't tell anyone will you please?"

"It's only me and Sheila here until late afternoon, so don't worry. Let's get Sheila in here." Pauline yells. "Sheila come into the office please."

Sheila walks in holing a strap on device, a black long one, and in a full black leather cat suit. "Hey what's up?'"

"Oh she's got G-spot Roger booked in."

Roger has been a regular for a long time and he loves to try pegging with all the girls. Even Pauline did him once.

"Sheila what is that face he makes when he climaxes?"

"I can't even look at him and this is my third time with him. He goes so red it's like watching a burns victim, suffering in pain. If it feels that great why isn't he displaying that on his face?"

Lisa joins in as she's seen him visit. "He scares me, I said no to servicing him. He doesn't like me I don't think, he looks so miserable."

"That's his face, all the time. I might ram this a little harder tonight, maybe I need to go deeper, see what reaction I get." Sheila says, seriously.

"Good luck with that one. I've known him years. You'd think he was at a funeral not a bloody sexually gratifying Parlour." Pauline has no faith in him changing.

"It's literally this." Pauline pulls the sides of her mouth downwards. "Like he's had a stroke."

This has settled Lisa's nerves, as she howls along with them. "Sheila I've got something to tell you, as if today can't get any funnier. I am being Maddie for a punter"

"Sorry, you what?" Sheila grinning as she's clipping on her strap on at the same time.

"Yep, I have point-blank lied on the phone to someone who was asking for the girl with disabilities, but she's not here, so I am gonna do him."

"But how?"

Lisa lets her legs go limp as she face plants the floor with her left side. "Like this, don't I look convincing! Now try and pick me up - pure dead weight. I would make a great Princess paraplegic."

Pauline and Sheila try lifting her as Lisa makes her whole body limp and this results in both of them falling on top of Lisa, in awkward positions; Pauline's face has landed into Lisa's breast and Sheila lands sideways so that the strap on is right on Lisa's face. The noise from all three crying with a hilarious and contagious sound is deafeningly loud. This goes on for sometime; stopping, starting to stand up, crying again, falling back over and deep breathing. Another moment Pauline adores - bonding with her girls.

The time rolls on, the punter is at the door for Sheila, it's Roger, for his pegging appointment. He pays Pauline with no smile, no spoken word, just a nod. Pauline is in a teasing mood, prodding Roger will be fun.

"Roger, I need to ask you a question."

Roger is all in black, jogging bottoms and top, about 65, face as miserable as fuck, has no underwear on, so can see his manhood clearly, looks terrified of speaking, but today Pauline is looking for entertainment.

"Soooo, Roger, with ya todger, when was the last time you cracked a smile?"

Roger in defence mode."Excuse me Polly, that's awfully rude."

"But you look so unhappy and miserable Rog!" Pauline thinking this will make him smile.

"That'll be because I had a stroke years ago, but thanks for the reminder that my face is fucked up Polly, really caring of you."

"Oh my God, I am soooo sorry, I really am. I was joking. You're not miserable, you have such kind feat....."

"Reign it back Polly. I don't want a compliment that's backed by sympathy, means nothing to me. Now if you'll excuse me, I'm having my other orifice taken care of. You should take a leaf out of your own book Polly." Roger throws her a filthy look and walks away.

"What the fuck is that supposed to mean?"

"International learning centre, it says outside. You haven't even learned how to be an english lady yet, let alone teach others any etiquette."

"Have you seen a classroom in here? This Parlour is for sex, the learning centre is code you knob." Pauline is grinding her teeth from side to side in a bid not to kick off fully. He has wound her up a treat.

"Now who looks like they are having a stroke. Backfire."

Roger's passing comment before entering the bedroom was one step too far for Polly. She loves money, good work ethics and a reputable establishment. Moments like these remind her of men who have talked down to her and a switch is flicked, a millisecond of an autopilot reaction, she sees red as fast as she approaches the bedroom and before she knows it she has him from behind, in a headlock, and drags him to the ground, drags him back out to reception, its all one big haze.

"EVER speak to me like that again you mother fucker, I will rip your throat out. Now get up and address me again in a manner I deserve, or you'll never step foot in here again."

Lisa and Sheila are now at their bedroom doors and watching in disbelief. They've seen Pauline kick off loads of times, but her eyes look darker, the expression is like she has left her body and watching down on this mad moment. She looks like a ball of angry energy, which could erupt and take on the world.

"Jesus Christ Polly, what the heck. I have heard you banter with clients many times, but never with me - you barely speak. I thought you were bantering with me. Fucking hell."

Roger looks at her and he sees she is not herself, something is happening. Lisa and Sheila dash towards her, she looks pale and as though she will faint. Roger puts his arm around her waist to prop her up and guides her to the stool, where she sits with his arm still holding her. A panic comes over her, some sort of anxiousness she's never experienced. Her head goes dark, the thoughts making her scared of losing her mind. Whatever just happened was a trigger, it set her mind to a place unfamiliar, breathing heavily, sweat dripping down her forehead and weakness never felt before. This throws Pauline totally off track, her eyes glaze over and her mind takes her to a memory of when she was 10 years old.

Pauline's memory bank unlocks a day when she was at home on her own, as Paul, his mum was out shopping and one of his mum's 'boy-friends' knocked the door. Paul looked through the curtains and recognised Mark, whom he named in his head as 'mackerel Mark', because he stank of fish. He always came on a Friday lunchtime, so he was baffled why he was at the door on a Thursday. Paul was dressed in boys clothes and happily skips to the door and greets him with a bright smile.
"Mummy is at the shops Mark."
In a friendly childlike tone, Mark opens a bag of sherbet lemons.

"Hello little man, want a sweet?"

Paul is thrilled at the sweets, his favourite, and takes two.

"Thank you so much. You usually come on a Friday don't you?"

Mark slides his foot into the doorway and picks him up.

"Yes, good boy, I do. But mummy asked me to call in on you as she's had to go somewhere."

Paul is still happy sucking on the sweets and feels comfortable, it felt like a daddy cuddle, which he hadn't ever had from his dad, who left 4 years prior to this day.

Mark's mood changes as he starts carrying him up the stairs. Paul takes the sweets out of his mouth and asks him why are they going upstairs. He places him on the bed and kneels down in front of him and puts his hand on his knee. With a serious face Mark tells Paul;

"I am about to teach you a thing or two, but it must be a secret, between me and you. If it isn't it will 'back-fire' and you'll be taken away into a children's home, no one will believe you, your mother will hate you, you'll have no one. This is our special time OK."

Paul starts to cry softly. Being dominated in this way plants a seed in his young mind, one that becomes powerful in its growth when needing to use denial, detachment & disassociation later in life. Mark's dirty hands upon him was terrifying and once he had finished with Paul he reiterated his warning; "Tell anyone and it will backfire."

The burying of this memory was something so forgotten about, and a shock to the system, because here it is 30 years later, resurfacing just from a word, the trigger of 'backfire', a simple word in a tense situation was all it took to explode.

Pauline is sitting down and regulating her breath to a level where she is slipping back into the here and now.

With a quiver in the side of her cheek she quietly whispers,

"What just happened?" She's shaking and wondering if she's having a stroke.

Everyone is silent, not knowing what to say, giving her space and also scared to see this strong powerful woman in a vulnerable state. Lisa rubs her back, Roger sits on the floor, Sheila kneels down beside Pauline.

When Pauline is 'back in the room' the sudden new memory of abuse engulfs her and takes her breath away, but she decides to keep that to herself, drinks water and decides a 10mg valium will relax her head as it feels noisy, disturbed, unbalanced and echoing from every sound around her.

Pauline gives them a different version of what she was experiencing because telling the truth at this moment may take her to a darker space and that is a place she doesn't want to go.

What just happened was deep enough and darker than ever, so to highlight that could be catastrophic in Pauline's mind, so she graces them with an afterlife story.

"I felt weird, dizzy and light. I could see this light, really bright, in a tunnel. I could see my dog from when I was a child. I think I just saw what the walkway to heaven is like. I can't explain it. All I could hear was - go back...go back. So I did."

"Wow, oh myyyy God. There was a documentary on the other night about people having near death experience's, this sounds just like it. This is wild." Sheila says as she's standing up.

Pauline starts laughing at Sheila. "How can I take you serious with a strap on in my face."

Sheila totally forgetting she has this strapped to her but keeps her composure as if standing proud. Making it more attractive to the punter present, as he will be pounded by this thick black 11" Pegasus shortly.

Roger forces a small smile, all that he can manage to anyway, and seems glad Pauline is ok, because he's not good with illnesses and drama, so he's relaxing back into why he is there and apologises to Pauline and she apologises.

"Roger I think you just witnessed the hand of God touching me and letting me know everything is going to be ok, and that I am looked over by Angels and my dog."

"I feel a discount coming on." Roger sneaks in.

"Piss off, you should be paying me more. Here, feel this." Pauline extends her hands.

"This skin has touched God, it'll bring you good luck back, tenfold, trust me. If you want wealth, success and health, then paying me more will increase all of those elements in your life." Pauline is reeling this off like she has special powers, even Lisa and Sheila are looking at her oddly, wondering if she means it.

Pauline winks at Roger. "Bless you. I forgive'th. Thou shan't bestow upon thee anything other than succulent forbidden fruits which thou shall be allowed to devour without judgement or foolery, that casts no darkness upon thee."

Pauline is licking her lips, but it doesn't come across as seductive, more like a thirsty deranged cat."

It's silent. Lisa mimes to Sheila; "Shall we call an ambulance?"

The indication from Sheila's shrugged shoulders gives her nothing to go on, so takes action. Lisa throws a glass of water over Pauline's face and calls her name loudly. "POLLY."

Pauline jolts as if she has been out of her body or not quite with it.

"I'm ok, don't panic. Sorry, I was daydreaming, I think. Right let's get to work. Roger don't try taking the piss out of me when I am in a vulnerable state like that, asking for discounts."

"I wasn't, honestly I was trying to cheer you up. With all honestly I didn't know what to say, I felt awkward. Are you going to be alright? You look like the colour is coming back, you looked like you were not in there, if that makes sense."

"No fuss please, I am fine."

Pauline walks off to office, Sheila and Roger go back into bedroom, Lisa goes back to check on Pauline.

"Polly that scared me, are you sure you're fine? It didn't look like you were in there, what was happening? You really feel it was some kind of connection to the afterlife?"

"Don't be daft, of course not. I wanted to wind Roger up. But something did happen to me before I came out with all that heavenly talk. An old memory came flying into my mind, childhood stuff, I wasn't going to tell him that though, it's something I need to process on my own."

"Of course, and you know you can share with me whenever."

"I know, thank you. Time you got on that bed and put your legs in some kind of convincing way." Pauline kisses her on the forehead. "I love you."

Lisa is stunned to hear this and stands frozen and part open-mouthed as Pauline leaves the room.

Lisa hasn't heard anyone ever tell her they love her, never. This feeling she wants to capture, smiles and holds that space for a minute, Pauline's three words will do more for her than she will ever know. A tear comes to Lisa's eye, she's happy, this is something she will hold dear until she dies.

Twenty minutes later the man for 'Maddie' has arrived, Pauline checks Lisa is ready, Lisa says five minutes, so lets him in and takes his money and strikes up conversation to give Lisa a few minutes. This well-spoken man in beige chino's, an untucked pink shirt and boating shoes, wouldn't look out of place drinking beer at the Cambridge & Oxford boat race. A bit 'la-dee-dah' however, extremely pleasant and a huge smile for Pauline. There's a look from them both, into each other's eyes, a little flirtatious on both parts.

"Phwaoorr, I wish I booked you now."

"What made you choose our disability dish?"

"I like TOTAL control, trapping someone, doing what I want, makes me rock hard. Think it stems from when I walked in on my dad doing it to my cousin. She was in a body brace after an accident at the fairground as she wasn't strapped in properly, and overweight, so she flew off the top of that fucking roller coaster into the air, and I laughed for days. The sight of her up there, with the moon behind her like a fat E.T, just cracked me up. Then obviously I felt guilty when I was told she would be bed bound, in a body brace with no way of knowing for a while if she would recover properly."

"That must have been awful?"

"For me, or for her?"

"Henry you're so naughty."

"Got to be truthful." Henry laughs and tells his tale as if he is immensely proud. Pauline studies his face, in somewhat disbelief, but is used to obscure stories, which fascinates her.

"I was hungry one night, Beth, my cousin, was staying with us in a special bed in our dining room for a few weeks. I walked in and there was my dad pumping away at her, with a gag in her mouth and I was hooked. So I did it the next night, then the next, then my dad walked in on me and went ballistic, calling me a dirty little pervert and that he was going to tell my mum. I couldn't stop laughing, the more angry he got and the more he shouted, made me howl as I knew I had him by the balls because he could not get me in trouble, because I had seen him do it. So I had the trump card and knew I could do it more and he would not be able to tell on me. It's that where the turn on came from I reckon."

"Wow, that's some deep shit mate. I've heard some tales in my time but that's top 3. I take it you didn't carry on with Beth, did you?"

"I was loving the full powerful charge I had over my father. It was alien to me and there was a certain rush going through my body and this new-found dominance sparked a desire in me I never knew I had. I had the key to his future; I could tell mum and he would lose her and the house, or we come to an agreement - luckily he got on board."

"What was the agreement?"

"That we would take it in turns."

"That poor girl." Pauline says with her hand on her chest.

"She was 21, not a girl. I was 16. She could have said no."

"Could she speak?"

"Well, no, not at the time, more gurgling. She can talk now though."

"Still, so sad." Pauline realises she's just judged him and she prides herself on being open-minded and un-shockable. "But hey ho, I hope she is ok and that you are happy. Look after her in there, she suffered terribly in a car crash, she's ever so fragile."

"Don't you worry Madame, she's in safe hands. And yeah, Beth is fully recovered, but we don't speak."

"Because of what happened?"

"Kind of. She told me she preferred my dad shagging her, so I cut the cord, she can fuck off."

"You seem a bit angry about that."

"Honestly, I treated her well; fed her, went shopping for her and even let my mate fuck her one night. She's so ungrateful."

Pauline is put off a little. "You can go on through now, was really nice to meet you...I forgot to ask your name?"

"Henry. And ditto. Polly?"

"That's me, Polly the proprietor of the plushest Parlour in this city."

"Cute, very cute. See you shortly pretty Polly."

Henry enters the bedroom. Pauline decides to check in on the new girls.

CHAPTER NINE

Upstairs

Whilst all is in order, Polly's Parlour 2 has been thriving. Emma and Julia have been covering day and night, so Pauline decides to pop up and check in. She does knock the door, but no one answers and she can hear a TV on, so lets herself in.

Jake is on the floor, passed out, with a stack of call cards on his lap, so he will be immediately in the firing line as soon as she has explored what else lurks in this odd atmosphere. In one bedroom is Emma and Julia, asleep, Sheila's room is occupied by two women asleep naked together and the last room is a girl who's sat up on side of bed, with a wad of cash next to her. Pauline is not happy.

"Who the fuck are you?"

Megan is a she-male, a name everyone uses when someone has organs of both. She has bleached cornrow hair, a large Adam's apple, stands up in her bra and Y-fronts, squares up to Pauline in a very deep voice.

"I'm Megan, who the fuck are you disturbing my peace?"

"You're looking at the owner of this place."

Pauline stands with her arms folded, waiting for that

information to sink in for Megan.

"Oh, excuse me, sorry, I crashed after my shift."

"Where do you work?"

"Here, started couple days ago. Julia said you agreed to it."

"Did she now?" Pauline is seething.

"How much you made so far?"

"About 600."

Pauline walks over to the bed side cabinet and picks up the cash, licks her finger, then counts out £300 and puts it in her bra."

"Hey, I have already given Julia £100, leaves me with fuck all."

"Let's get one thing straight, it's a 50/50 split, in time that changes and you'll get 60%, plus tips. For now you pay me and no one else. Do I make myself clear?"

"Sure, I totally get it. I only went by what the girls told me."

"Which was?"

"You were looking for extra staff. I am popular in this field, punters love that I have tits with my meat still intact downstairs - it's big money."

As Pauline was in that same position years ago, she knows Megan is speaking truthfully.

"I will chat to you later, I am not angry at you, but at that fucking Julia I am."

Pauline breezes out of the room and back into the bedroom where Julia and Emma are sleeping. Pauline slams the door behind her and Emma half open her eyes. Pauline grabs Julia by the arm and shakes her to wake her up. Emma looks sketchy and shaking.

"Julia, wake up."

Julia is snappy and angry she's been woken. A morning person she is not, far from it.

"It's my day off, what do you want?"

"I want some money and I want it now."

Pauline sees her handbag on the floor and picks it up and empties it on the bed. Make-up, used tissue, three pound in coins, and £40 in notes is all she has.

"I shall take this and hand it to Megan, now get up and get yourself ready, you are not having today off, you will work this afternoon and pay back Megan the remaining £60."

Julia tries to interrupt but Pauline raises her voice.

"Don't speak over me Julia, ever." Pauline points her finger into Julia's face. "Fuck with me like that one more time and...."

Julia is not a pushover, she grew up in a rough estate in London, she's only in Brighton because she had to leave London for her own safety, no one knows this. In her cockney accent Julia jumps out of bed and clenches her fists.

"You wanna go Pauline? Let's fucking av it."

Pauline mimics Julia. "Let's av it. What are you 12? Grow up."

Pauline stands up and goes nose to nose with Julia. Paulines's eyes go black, leaning her head forward, pushing Julia back by her forehead.

"Think very carefully about your next move, Julia, choose wisely."

Julia feels like she's over a barrel, has nowhere to go and this a perfect hiding place, a nice home and good money. Usually Julia would be in the back of a police car by now, her temper is off the scale and she would have had this wrapped up, opponent on the floor and been arrested.

A fight between these two would be carnage and both as hard as each other. Somehow Julia manages to centre herself and remind herself she will lose everything unless she turns this around. This kills her inside, to back down from confrontation, but she forces herself to do it.

"I apologise, it won't happen again."

"Too fucking right it won't happen again. That is my final warning. I don't care what time of the of day or night it is, I will throw you out if I so much as get a whiff of bullshit from you."

Pauline has barely blinked the whole time, her eyes fixated on studying Julia's eye contact and body language.

"Pauline, hands up, I screwed up. Sorry"

"Appreciate the apology. Now, Emma, let this be a lesson to you too. You knew this was going on, I will be keeping my eye on you as well."

Emma nervous, "I didn't know..."

"DON'T try and play me Emma. Both of you are on probation. You have a month to prove to me you can work hard, make me money and be transparent. I can sense dishonesty a mile off. Be genuine and you'll go a long way, especially with me. If you think you can't handle the pace, pack your bags right now."
Julia and Emma fall silent, Emma bows her head, Julia gets back into bed.

"Right, that settles it then. I will let Adam's apple do some trial shifts for me. She seems cool."

Emma relieved Pauline has calmed down. "Yeah she is lush, that Adam's apple is rather large innit?"

Pauline talks quietly.

"I can imagine she looks glam done up with make up on. There's plenty of calls for half and half lately."

"Yeah she can make mega bucks I reckon."

"Who do the lesbians belong to?"

"Jake's mates."

Pauline starts to exit the bedroom, as she holds onto the handle, about to open it, turns to the girls.

"Oh, and just for the record Julia, if we did have a fist fight you would be in an ambulance right now. Don't underestimate me."
Pauline cackles as she leaves because she was a fighter in her day, in pubs and clubs, with men and women, but feels over that nowadays. Somewhere deep in her gut she still has that fire though, if need be.

Julia looks at Emma. "Pfftt, I'd bang her right out. In an

ambulance? She's tripping mate."

"I reckon she's tough, I wouldn't mess with her." Julia snares and turns her back on Emma's comment and pulls a blanket over herself. Emma closes her eyes.

Pauline was outside the door listening. She rolls her tongue around her teeth and holds herself back from charging back in, she decides keep this to herself.

Pauline goes back to the room with the entangled girl duo. "Oooiii, Mel & Kim, get up."

Jemma and Clare are what's described as 'lipstick lesbians' on the scene; not butch, wear make up, look fem and pretty. Jemma is the fiercest out of the two, and stirs more.

"Beg your pardon lady? Mel is dead."

Pointing to her fast asleep partner. "She looks like her, bloody state of it. Get dressed and come join me in the lounge, bring the dead one with you."

Jemma is far from shocked usually, but this has her mouth open wide and stumped.

Pauline has walked off to the lounge.

When Pauline is joined by them in the lounge, Megan has already woken Jake up, so Pauline takes a seat.

"Never seen you look so rough before Jake, what are you doing in here?"

Jake rubs his eyes and explains. "I tried that Ketamine, it blew my mind. I was actually anchored to this arm chair, like a dead body. If it can knock a horse out then no wonder I was so trashed, never again. Sorry Polly, I could not make it outside but I will do a round of cards in a bit."

Pauline warmly advises Jake. "I worry about you darling, you don't need drugs. You have amazing energy, good-looking, smart, drugs will ruin you."

"I know, I know, I am quitting all drugs, just have a smoke. I need my money, that was a one off."

"I bloody hope so."

"Megan here's £40, Julia has been told to pay you back the remaining £60 later. You can work here, but everything goes through the appointment book downstairs. If it's a walk in off the street, you still need to ring it down and let us know. At the moment most of the clientele is off the street, I need to know who they are and that you are all safe, always."

Megan seems half pleased. "I thought it was a live in job?"

"It can be Megan. The room you've been in is up for rent, pay me extra for the room at the end of the month."

"Ah, that's music to my ears, thank you ever so much. I have been on people's sofa's for a year, this will help me get my life back on track."

"I can imagine the phone will be hot when new cards go out. Let's think of what kind of card we can put out for you. Let's get creative"

Pauline looks at the girls. "You two work?"

Jemma and Clare had a sandwich shop but it closed down when Gregg's bakery set up next door. Jemma put a brick through the window and got in trouble for criminal damage. Clare is at college part-time doing hair and beauty but doesn't like it because it costs money and they are skint. They are in a position of needing money.

"We are both broke right now to be honest."

"How do you feel about voyeurism?"

Clare has never heard of it. "Is that the new ship docked in Southampton?"

Everyone but her knows, breaking the tenseness in the room as they all laugh.

Pauline finds it endearing. "That's the cutest answer ever! No, it's when people watch people having sex, no touching, just watching."

"Oh. People do that?"

Jake tells her. "Clare there's good money in it. Pay your college fees no trouble."

"You mean watch me and my girl?" Jemma asks.

"Yep, I need some specials on Polly's menu and it's gaining a lot of interest, especially with gay girls. Use that room, set some chairs at the side and do appointment only sex shows."
Jemma and Clare look at each other and say nothing.
"Think about it."

"You should so do it girls." Jake encourages his mates. "You'd be ace at it. Wear a mask if you don't want people look at your faces."

"And wigs if you want." Pauline offers. "Be nice to have some variety, expanding is good for business."

Holding hands the girls muter to each other, then turn to Pauline. "Yes ok, we'll do it."

"Welcome to Polly's Parlour 2. Start tomorrow. And Megan?"

Megan's excited "YEESS" sounds like an opera singer at his lowest vibration.
All three are excited and discussing what they can do. Jake is happy as more work for him with extra cards, laundry, meaning more hours and money.

"Handy man here for all your needs ladies."

"Thanks Jake, get yourself ready I want a fresh load of cards today." Pauline sits down to get creative and asks for their input.
Jemma asks; "Can you put us down as Mel & Kim?"

Megan is shocked. "Wow, that's a great idea."

Pauline quickly address that. "My idea and yes it is genius. Let's get to work."

Lisa is loving her appointment. As soon as he walked into her bedroom she looked at his eyes, a feeling of familiarity came over her and made her feel at ease. She has been washed and changed by Henry, now he is wrapping the straps around her to

lift her into the hoist, with great difficulty. Lisa has made her body go totally limp and is playing the character brilliantly.
"Time for sucky sucky Maddie."

He undoes his trousers and grabs Lisa by the throat, gently, and controls her head movement as she starts sucking him off.

Pauline comes back through the front door and puts some music on medium volume and sits at reception.
As Henry is enjoying himself he leans over and opens the sash window telling Lisa he needs air.
She has her mouth full so mutters "OK" as best she can.
Moving position has given Lisa cramp in her left hip and leg, but is supposed to be paralysed so cannot do anything but suffer. To mask this, Lisa starts to moan and groan as though Henry is really hitting the spot. Through being gagged by his cock, Lisa is making the most extraordinary noises. Henry is looking on with a confused frown but carries on. He sees the curtain twitch a few moments later and a head with a balaclava is watching on. Henry knows him and does not mind him watching, he almost gets off on it. Henry forces his dick deep into her mouth. As soon as Lisa has swallowed his load, the man at the window climbs in and Lisa looked terrified. Henry puts his finger to her lips.
"Sshh, not one fucking whimper from you."
Henry's mate is fully indoors now, takes his balaclava off and Lisa feels like she knows him, now feels like she knows both, but can't remember where from in the moment of pure horror and fear.
"Where's the money? Henry asks Lisa.
She knows in this room is Pauline's money, that she's been saving for quite some time. Pauline has been saying she and Robert are travelling round the scottish coastal roads in a camper van after Gary's funeral, something they've both wanted, so her money is important. But Lisa is petrified and moves her eyes to the left and nods in the same direction.
"Behind that sideboard?" Henry asks.

Lisa whispers, "Yes."

Henry tells his mate, Dave, to keep an eye on her. Dave laughs. "What do you think she's going to do - wheel herself out of here in this?"
Dave grabs Lisa's left leg up high and drops it. "Look, lifeless. You aren't going anywhere are you sweetheart."

Lisa has never felt so handicapped, laying legs spread in mid-air whilst the Parlour's little weak safe is a money box with a padlock, in a hole in the wall, behind the cabinet, which is being wrenched open.

The last thing Pauline wants is the tax office stinging her, so a lot goes through unaccounted for. Her accountant is as dodgy as they come and she keeps HMRC off her back and lives a comfortable lifestyle, with stocks and shares and some savings, this box is what she has been putting by for a few years, Lisa feels sick they are raiding her.

She watches Dave's eye's again and it clicks, the terror sets in, it's the two thugs who raped her mum. Being in a wig and school uniform, masses of make up, freckles and glasses, Lisa is unrecognisable to them in this criminal storm before her.

Through fear, Lisa closes her eyes and prays they just leave out of the window.

As Henry wrenches the cash box open with a hammer he has with him, and puts all the cash in his jacket pocket, the door buzzer goes, bringing the room to a silence. Henry puts the hammer and cash tin aside, as he looks through crack of door. Lisa opens her eyes and looks at them both. They look worried, as if this isn't part of the plan.

"What do we do now"? Asks Dave, who's clearly the underdog between them both and does what he's told, a bit simple and vulnerable really, but also vacant, void of empathy for others.

Whispering aggressively, "Just shut up Dave. Let me listen."

Henry opens the door a jar and can see Pauline is buzzing someone in. He stands back, just one part of is eye looking. His nemesis, his bitter rival, over turf and drugs, is walking towards Pauline, it's Lee. Henry glares at Dave, Lisa sees fear in his eyes.

"It's that cunt Lee out there."

Dave's instant reaction is to charge forward, no thinking, just get Lee. The consequences could be fatal, Henry knows this, but he's playing it cool.

"Dave, Dave, look at me, straight at me buddy."

Henry knows he can bolt and no one can hold him back at times, he can sense Dave's tenseness needs to be intercepted immediately.

"Dave, calm, breathe with me, look at me."

He has Dave's attention and gets Dave to replicate what he is doing with calming down and chilling out with breathing. Lisa has no idea what's going on and accidentally hits the forward button and the hoist collapses with her weight and movement. Dave and Henry put both of their hands over their mouths to stop the laughing fit which is on the tip for both of them, making it one of the hardest times in their lives to hold such a feeling in.

Lisa is on the floor and keeps her eyes closed. She wants to pop her eyes out of her head through shock then she hears Dave ask Henry;

"Think Lee knows about the coke?"

She's now sure, she's positive, they are the ones who killed Gary and took the coke. The emotional rush in Lisa is overwhelming but she keeps her eyes closed and tries to calm herself.

Thankfully Pauline, chatting with music on in the background, means she did not hear Lisa's fall from Grace. They know brothels make money and that there will be cash at reception and they want it badly. Booking Maddie meant they would get control of the Parlour, knowing if Lisa appears it would not matter as she hasn't seen their faces before, a new plan is hatched and she told them this was her day off.

Lisa is listening whilst pretending to be unconscious.

"What the fuck is he doing here?"

Shrugging his shoulders at Dave. Henry thinks, rubs his head. "Wait for a few minutes, I have still got 45 minutes left of this appointment so.... calm."

Pauline is leaning over the glass top curved reception desk, subtly being flirty, Lee trying hard not to gaze at her with a glint in his eye. Pauline knows this is dangerous, but being on his good side is a survival technique she has frequently used; knowing how to make sure that no-one should suspect her for anything.

Lee may not have retrieved the coke but he certainly does not think Pauline had anything to do with it anymore, she's been too honourable to him and now the initial grief is less, he's tired, and likes to confide in Pauline as it was his brother's last connection, he feels close to Gary when around her. Now the dust has settled, she is more relaxed with him and asking Pauline about what she would like to be described as in Gary's upcoming eulogy and memories to share at the service. Pauline reflects and looks happy and starts to write on a piece of paper.

Henry and Dave take their chance as Pauline is leaning away from the direction of Maddie's door and Lee has his full back turned to the bedroom.

Lisa is left on the floor as Dave turns psychotic.

"Hands above your head. Don't turn around, knees to the floor."

Pauline glances over, only one second needed to see he has a gun in his hand. Pauline's chin starts to tremble, Lee is hit over the head with the gun and drops to the floor but is not knocked out. He sits, leaning against the wall, holding his head and is warned by Henry to keep his eyes closed, produces a tie out off his pocket, and shuts off Lee's vision.

"Hand all the cash over."

Pauline, advises them - "Guys, please, this is my livelihood."

"Give me it, now." Demands Henry.

Pauline keeps her mouth closed, the valium has been the perfect smoother for this day, opens the till calmly and lets Dave stash the contents into a bag. Pauline watches with sadness, in disbelief this is happening to her. Henry is being impatient with Dave.

"Fucking hurry up."

Dave is filling his pockets with sweets and condoms from the jars on reception, puts a lolly in his mouth.

"What's the rush? There's a cripple in one room and these two are captive, let's root around the other rooms. May as well mate."

One of the bedroom doors opens and it's Sheila with her strap on, her client has sneaked out of the window to go to the call box up the road, sees the gun and holds her hands up in the air as the rubber cock swings about. In disbelief Henry flicks it, slaps it, laughs at her. Dave checks the bedroom, no one in there. Sheila sees Lisa poke her head slightly out, hides her panic and steps to the front of Henry, so his back remains facing Maddie's room.

In Maddie's room, Lisa has unclipped herself. Somehow Lisa has dug deep to gain the courage to even stand up, let alone be thinking she can help or protect Pauline. For every time Pauline has made Lisa feel wanted, loved, heard and appreciated, this feels like payback, a huge favour, to give something back, but what at this point she is not sure. Shaking and boiling up with a fearful rush, Lisa closes her eyes, tilts head back and leans against the wall to think. This move has only come because she knows they think she is disabled and 99% sure they don't need to come back and check on her in a hurry.

Dave shouts out from Pauline's room. "Bingo mate, come on here, loads of jewellery."

Lisa knows what jewellery she has and knowing there is a special piece she bought Pauline for her birthday, and cost a bit of money, winds Lisa up. Henry's hammer is on the side, Lisa has no other option, this is the tool to keep her safe. Lisa opens the door a little and manages to mouth to Sheila; "Get ready to take Lee's blindfold off."

Sheila looks petrified and puts her face to the floor.

"Bring it out here Dave, can't bring these three with me."

As Dave arms himself with a box and a bag, Lisa gets ready to pounce. Everyone has only ever seen a sweet side to Lisa, but who she is in this moment is a woman full of anger, a woman who feels like she could kill because of what they did to her mum.

As Dave walks down the corridor, towards reception, Lisa tip toes behind and the cries of her mum in her head force her to smash the hammer over his back and give one kick to Dave's lower spine. Dave falls into Henry. Both fall over Lee and onto the front door entrance, with gun sliding on the floor.

Sheila, shaking like a leaf, pulls the tie from Lee's face. Lee gets a chance to pick up the gun and take control of the situation. Lee gets his bearings, stands back and can't believe his eyes.

"Well look who it is - the bent brothers, Harry and Dean from the whitehawk estate. What the fuck are you playing at, morons."
Lee introduces them to the girls.

"Biggest pair of losers you'll ever meet ladies, these two are always getting caught up in shit and sometimes avoiding jail, everyone knows you both grass to avoid time inside. Empty your pockets, both of you."

Between them they have all of Pauline's money, a bag of weed, a small knife, coins and keys. Lee asks Sheila to pick it all up.

Lisa needs to say something, it is her reclaiming her power after what she just been subjected to and witnessed. Lisa takes Pauline's hand and kisses it.

"Shock, you gave false names, we've not heard that before. I couldn't let them take this haul from you Polly, no way." Lisa kisses her on their forehead.

With the biggest gloating expression ever, Lisa walks towards Harry and Dean and pulls her wig & glasses off, then wipes her lipstick with her cuff and introduces herself.
"Hello again boys."
Their looks of being dumbstruck at her reveal is worth a million to Lisa.

"You know these guys?' Lee asks.

"I've had the displeasure of meeting these two, hooded & tooled up, threatening to kill my mum. This fat pig brutally forced himself on my mum yesterday, in front of me."

Lee is furious to hear this and smashes the gun against Dean's head.

"Looks like it's payback boys." Lisa is revelling in this. "Where's my money?"

Harry confesses to her. "Spent some, rest is at home."

The sound of police sirens in the distance start getting louder. Good old Roger rang them, looking out for Sheila because she's his anal angel, he has to protect her and anonymously report from a call box, he's a member of parliament, so wise to run and report.

Lisa adds more.

"There's plenty more Lee, these two knew Gary, they discussed if you knew it was them when referring to coke."

Lee's rage builds up, his eyes tearing up, it's clicked; they had beef with Gary years ago, they are the ones who ended Gary's life, he's sure of it. Pointing the gun at them both, Lee is only focused on them, the outside noise is not bringing him out of this fixation. Pauline slides her hand onto his, both holding and pointing the gun together. The sirens are outside, Pauline moves towards the front and faces Lee and the Gun.

"Don't let them ruin your future, put it down, the police are here, Lee, please."

Lee slowly relaxes into reality when the knocking at the door is loud, with the buzzer going at the same time. Lisa bravely steps past Harry and Dean on the floor, she opens the door.

The police say it was reported someone had broken their way in and threatening the girls.

Pauline recognises this policeman too, and he's one of the nice ones, they always get on, mainly because he pops in for a session occasionally and she always promises not to let anyone know. Naturally this policeman has Pauline's back and along with his colleagues, arrest Harry and Dean who have both tried kicking off, yelling their innocence and spitting at one of the policemen, adding to their charge sheet.

Lisa does not mention the rape at this moment, she needs to speak to her mum first. Lee informs them they've confessed to killing Gary, Pauline says she witnessed that confession, no mention of the gun, which is safely in Lee's back pocket and their belongings on the reception floor. When the commotion is settled and the police have gone, they all pick up the contents. Suddenly it dawns on them they haven't thanked Lisa. Pauline hits it out first.

"And holy shit girl, where did that feisty Madame come from? You saved us darling, you hero. I love you even more, thank you so much."

Lisa blushes." I had to do something, it came up from somewhere in me. Maybe I should do more Dominatrix work."

Pauline realises she's not told Lisa." Umm, you actually will be, starting next week."

"What do you mean?"

"That Teddy fella, I told him you would. Seeing how you've grown as a working girl, I think you'll be amazing at it."

Lisa feels pleased with herself and loves she has looked out for Pauline and her efforts are recognised. "You know what, yeah, I will be bloody brilliant."

"Perfect, Mistress Marilyn. That's your new name by the way."

"I absolutely love it, thank you, Polly."

"My pleasure darling. The big bucks will start rolling in for you when I am away. Work it girl."

Lisa has a new-found confidence. "Too right, I am looking forward to it."

Lee looks at her proudly too. "What a trooper, we owe you one." Lee picks up keys from the floor. "I know where he lives, I will go get what money is left."

"No Lee, you may get into trouble." Lisa replies with worry.

"I will do it now before the cops are all over his place, it's 5 minutes away. Trust me, this is the last part of the puzzle, full circle. I will bring back some champagne Polly."

Pauline looks exhausted and in need of a drink and gives Lee a tight hug, relieved it's all put to bed, and thanks him. The stress has left Pauline, and Lee. It's all been answered, the ending of this feels beautiful, light and free. Lee leaves and all three embrace.

"Me and my girls eh. Thank the lord I have you in my life. Robert, Harry and Dean were, sorry 'are' all connected to us, all scum and all had hatred for us, we did well, we won. Doesn't that feel great? To be a champion against dominating men for a change?"

Lisa and Sheila can feel that too. Girl power at its finest, Maddie will be proud, as long as the broken hoist is fixed and Lisa's cover not blown.

Lee returns with Moet Champagne and a carrier bag of goodies. Lee feels really pleased to hand Lisa two grand and rings, this means the earth to her, a favour which has put a lot of right in her head knowing she can hand the rings back to her mum, and money for some help. This should be able to pay for some therapy, counselling or treatment. What she saw her mother endure has pushed Lisa even further to support Maureen on a healing journey.

Lisa gives Lee a grateful hug, one more heartfelt than ever. Her heart has melted at this gesture. Lee kisses her on the nose and as he holds her waist.

"You deserve it."

Lee pops open the bubbly and pours them all a drink and makes a toast to Gary.
"To my bother, I hope you rest in peace now. To Gary."

The drinking continues, Pauline puts some music on and they all dance around the lounge, to 'flying without wings', Lee breaks down crying.
"God Polly, I miss him. I can't explain how I feel, the pain is there

but I feel we got him justice, so I feel at peace, it's weird."

"I miss him too. His funeral in two days, he will be looking down on us, proudly."

"He bloody better be." Pauline taps his glass with hers.

"He will, trust me."

Matthew pulls up outside in the camper van he's bought for their little trip around the coast in a couple of days. Pauline goes out and sits in there having a cup of tea with Matthew, who is loving treating Pauline and seeing how much she loves it. He gets a map out and has put felt tip on the journey they are going on. As he's excited telling her and looking at the map, she is looking at him from the side, fancies him even more today.

"Matthew you are gorgeous. I like that you don't walk around thinking that and being so humbled and understated."

Matthew, is as sharp as can be. "Who said I don't think that? I am proper London fashion week model material. I can't quite believe I have been given this face, just stunning Polls."

Pauline spills her tea because he's so dry, and his straight face does not crack. Pauline even feels he may mean it. "You are kidding right?"

"I can't fathom how you find that a joke. Gods gift some might call it."

He's wound her up too long, he breaks the stern face and his eyes let her know he was being playful. Matthew has no ego, he's gentle, patient, witty, interesting to talk to and treats her like she is unique.

Pauline can sense the realness and the past issues of turning someone down because of their clothes, or shoes, or crooked teeth, didn't mean it was those things to put her off at all. In this camper van she can see it's the person you fall in love with, not what they have or wear, if the electrical current is there when you touch, its game over; none of that matters. The eyes connect, the sexual tension sparks another feeling, the kiss seals the deal, all wrapped in one is this - Matthew.

Pauline has finally fallen in love and felt it in her heart for the first time in her life. Euphoric emotions, goose bumps on the skin are felt by both. Pauline stands up, Matthew takes her hand and spins her around under his arm, asks her to twirl again, she willingly spins and falls into his chest. Matthew's big hands take her by the side of the neck, a hot skin hold, pulls her towards him and kisses her perfectly and doesn't want to let go.

"I love loving you, Polly."

Since being little, to hear those words, for a man to admit he loves her for who she is, accepting her transparency, is what she prayed for. Voicing that in therapy has given her palpitations. To witness it, Matthew showing her his heart, washes away so much of the past which hurt her. Here she feels real, that she's enough and can truly be herself. Pauline sits down and lets her body feel this intense emotion, one she has longed for. She feels like the woman she has always yearned for. Even though things have been rough, life feels pretty perfect right here in this moment.

CHAPTER TEN

Closure

During the third session with her counsellor, which Terry has crammed in for her due to her leaving soon, means she's had two sessions in this one week, but she has loved it.

Pauline says she feels better and knowing she is going off on a month road trip with Matthew she feels she can 'move on' and is open with Terry.

"Three sessions and already I feel stronger. Can I come back for more after my trip if I feel I need it?"

Terry complies with her wish - with a question; "What would you feel most drawn to, if coming back?"

"You mean what would I like to talk about?"

Terry nods.

"I think my dad. My mum made it clear by her final letter what was between us and I got to say goodbye regardless. My dad leaving was abrupt and no answers or a goodbye. I don't think I've made my peace with that. I feel like it's the last piece of the puzzle perhaps. Be nice to check and see if I am holding onto it, how deep and how to let it go."

"I think that's a good mindset to have and worth checking in with that if you want to when you return. Sometimes just saying goodbye, whether that's verbal, written, or thought, is enough to make your peace with it. I would gladly support you in that."

Pauline feels a bit upset to stop here.

Terry can sense why, or has an idea. "You know the therapeutic relationship can be a very comforting and letting it go can trigger the feelings around loss."

"You can read me well can't you?"

"I get a good sense of who you are. I believe you will continue to make progress in here, and out in the world. Thank you for being open and sharing your life with me. It's a privilege, truly."

Pauline gives him a firm handshake and looks into his eyes, silence falls, Pauline gets goosebumps. "Thank you for letting me be me, for getting me on the road to healing. I feel blessed. Thank you so much."

"My absolute pleasure Pauline."

Pauline leaves but sits on the doorstep and takes a moment to reflect on who she was when she walked through that door two weeks ago and how she's leaving now. Proud of her own success is a feeling not often felt, but here she is bursting in the heart to scream it from the roof tops. Lee is on her side, being with Matthew feels right, road trip ahead, Polly's Parlour and Polly's Parlour 2 are doing well, the girls are happy, therapy is working...it's a great day. This shows in the way she stands up and strides off like she's on cloud nine. This night she sleeps like never before; 10 hours of peaceful sleep.

Waking up fresh has given Pauline a clear head to sort business affairs. Two days ago she let everyone know she will be having a staff meeting and all must attend. Pauline feels it'll be the perfect opportunity to let the girls know Layla is safe and well and will be returning to work, it will be all hands on deck whilst she is away and rings the guest house to check in on her and give her the news she can return to Polly's Parlour.

Pauline speaks to her mate Karen, who runs it.

"Hey Karen, how's life darling?"

Karen is late 50's, loud, bleached blonde and always been there for Pauline. "Hey doll, how are ya?"

"Life is looking sweet. Let's do lunch and catch up soon, it's been a while. Maybe Layla could join."

"Would love that, yes. Who's Layla?"

Pauline's heart sinks.

"Maybe she checked in under a different name. Two days ago, Layla was checking in to yours, I sent her up to you."

"Been fully booked for weeks Polly, no one new checked in here."

"Are you sure?"

"Yep, just me here on my own at the minute."

Pauline would love to hold her rage in but she flips.

"That little bitch has done me over again. Just you wait until I find her. Karen, I am furious, gotta go."

Usually Pauline has nice telephone manners, especially with friends like Karen, but her mood means she slams the phone down with force and no goodbye. She takes many deep breaths to compose herself, ready for her team meeting, but it's left a sour taste in her mouth.

Parlour 2 has been busy with the girls working long hours, so decided to get them all together for a welcome break. She also wants to get them inspired when they hold the fort properly, when she goes away, and make them feel appreciated.

Slowly they arrive, Pauline looking at her watch and raising her eyebrow as its 11.58 and she said 12 - a stickler for time. Julia, Emma, Jake, Meg, Sheila & Andy are all in lounge, Lisa, Maddie and Natalie were already there, just Sandra and Leigh to arrive, which they do at 12.03. Pauline announces one word abruptly;

"Punctuation."

Leigh not in the mood for anyone today. "Not into mathematics, so dunno what you're saying."

Pauline taps her watch forcefully.

"It's English. It means be-on-fucking-time." Pauline is taking her anger out on Leigh, no particular reason, she feels Leigh is too cocky at times, so Pauline is gunning for her today.

Leigh rolls her eyes, Sandra apologies. All three walk to the lounge.

"Right, now that everyone is *finally* here, let's crack on."

Leigh grins and shakes her head. Pauline puts the Parlour's diary, pen and filofax down on the side, crosses her arms and stares at Leigh. The room was a vibe, chatting and laughing, all pleased to be on a break, now it's just low talking, people sensing a change in atmosphere. Pauline puts her hand up and 'shhhhh's' the room.

"Stand up." Leigh looks around thinking she's talking to someone else.

"Me?"

"Yep, up."

Leigh stands up and puts her hands in her pockets, chewing gum. "Problem Polly?"

"I did have - but I just got rid of it." Pauline points to the door. "Close it on your way out." A few people have gasped slightly, Jake giggles, the rest are open-mouthed.

"Are you being serious?"

No sound or movement from Pauline.

"Are you fucking joking Pauline?"

Pauline breaks her silence.

"EVER give me attitude again you will be out. One ounce of back chat, or pissing about when I am away I will get Andy to escort you out and that will be the last. Understood?"

Leigh biting her lip hard and swallows a lump in her throat, the lump of temper, and embarrassed to be called out in front of everyone, replies; "Cool, understood."

Pauline asserts her authority again. "Now sit down and shut up."

Leigh sinks into a bean bag and bites her nails.

"Right folks, the reason I have given you half a day off is because I want you all to come together and look at rota's, and a list of jobs I've assigned to you all. It will be on the fridges of both apartments, so no forgetting what needs doing. I want this place running like clock work. Lisa is in charge and I will be ringing her once a week, or more, for a catch up and make sure you are all respecting my business. Are we all clear?"

The room erupts with "YES" from all.

"Today I want you all to spring-clean, a bit of painting in some rooms, Jake and Andy if you could please. Jake smiles through gritted teeth, Andy would do anything for Pauline, so that's a given.

Upstairs needs the attention so she needs everyone to sort this so she can go away knowing all maintenance and jobs are all completed.

"Emma and Julia can you go into town and buy new sheets and towels, oils and wipes please?"

Both agree. Emma whispers to Julia. "We could nick all that and keep the money." Julia nudges her in the ribs and tells her to be quiet, but agrees.

Jake has been helping them a lot with laundry, cards in call boxes, shopping and company for the girls in between clients, so praises him. Andy promises to do 5 nights a week and has a mate who can get on board and do security too, Pauline trusts Andy to make that decision.

"I want to say a huge thank you for all the commitment you have shown, the hours you have put in. You've cost me a fortune in lube, but you're all worth it."

The room is cheerful, with all in good spirits.

"This place, and upstairs, is not only my business, it's my home. You are all welcome here. Just, please, look after it won't you? It's a wild world out there, the more we stick together and work as a team, life will be brighter. You're my little family."

Pauline has a tear in her corner of her eye but her lightening bolt reaction to turn to the side and wipe it whilst picking her mug up, means no one saw it. Pauline has all the tricks up her sleeve when it comes to masking emotions.

Lisa stands up. "Polly, don't you fret, I will have this place in order and we will all work together as a team. Thank you for everything you do for us. Lisa starts to sing - "For *she's* a jolly good fellow."
The room joins in, even a couple of little harmonies, which Pauline points out, with a hand on her chest. She feels loved, valued and at peace here. Hugs all, even Leigh, room bursting with noise, as they all chip in to sort rota as Pauline sorts the money out for them.

"OK, so now that's all sorted, have a great day. I will take bookings from 8pm for upstairs and down, that gives you a few hours free time too."

When everyone has gone Pauline is over come by internal anger, Layla has pushed her buttons one too many times. Whilst pausing for thought, she catches Lisa before she leaves.
"Come with me."

Lisa startled that she's grabbed her arm and started to make her walk anyway. "What the hell Polly."

"'Trust me, I will tell you on the way." Pauline lets go of Lisa arms and they walk up to the high street."

"Where are we going.?"

"That venomous Layla has done a runner."

"What, when? Where is she? You've seen her?"

"She tipped up, all emotional and running from Lee, pleaded her innocence and I gave her money towards a room, sent her up to my mates guest house. But guess what, she didn't check in. The only one that gossips around her is that Morgan at the sun-bed shop. Layla is often in there, she's bound to know something, so I need your help."

"How?"

"That minger Morgan won't tell me shit. She wanted to be one of my girls but I turned her down. We don't talk, but she tells you stuff. I need you to find out from her if any gossip on Layla."

"Oh, yeah, sure, she's a gossip queen."

"If she knows it's me she won't say anything, so I will have a sunbed and you chat. I will go in first and do 15 minutes on bed, you come in few mins after and chat, ok?"

"Polly, leave it with me. I'll do my best flirting."

"Oh, is she?"

"Yeah, been after me for ages."

"Perfect."

Pauline enters, Morgan is at reception, biting the side of her mouth, ignores Pauline.

Morgan has dyed black long straight hair, wears her managers badge with pride and dresses goth style, piercings all over her face and very blunt. Morgan has seen Pauline, she's pretending she hasn't.

Pauline taps her nails on the counter and lowers her voice. "I know you've seen me, I can see right through you."

Morgan flicks open a can of coke in Pauline's direction and takes a huge gulp. "Can I help you?"

"15 minutes I need." Pauline hands a £20 note to her.

"Full up, you'll have to wait."

"I can see a green light on bed 3, so cut the crap."

"It's broken. You look pale, I'd go for 30 minutes if I was you, Casper."

Pauline has been holding herself together, kept her cool, Morgan is testing her patience. Pauline grabs the lanyard round her neck and twists it so it gets tight on Morgans neck.

"Listen to me, Morticia Adams, sign me into that booth or I keep pulling this until...."

Lisa enters too early, acts shocked at the sight.

"Oh sorry Ladies."

Pauline lessens her grip, Morgan coughs a little and rubs her neck. Pauline is in the zone, she's staring at Morgan and not even acknowledging Lisa. Morgan takes her payment and gets her into booth 3. No words are spoken, just a tense atmosphere. Lisa comforts Morgan, knowing this is a good moment to get gossip, as she's got her whilst she's vulnerable.

"What the hell was going on there?"

"That dirty whore, hands all over me, for no reason."

Lisa rubs Morgans back. "Oh bless you, who is she?"

"She owns that brothel down the road. Loads of ugly tarts work for her. Yet she turns this down." Morgan points to her own face. "I would have made her loads."

Inside Lisa wants to lash out and let her know she works there, but gossip is too important and Lisa has always told her she works in a call centre, so she can never talk about Lisa being on the game, and makes it easy for her to get Morgan to talk.

"Sounds like you are better off not working for her if she's going to treat you like that. You're so beautiful Morgan."

Morgan is flattered and melts into Lisa's eyes. "Really? Me? Beautiful?"

"Yes, stunner, inside and out."

Morgan sits down, Lisa leans over the reception desk and gives Morgan the eye.

"So, any new goss".

Morgan looks around to make sure the coast is clear.
"Funny you should ask, it's to do with her in booth three."

"Do tell. I love your gossip. I don't know any of these people around here, so mum's the word, always."

Morgan half talks, half whispers.

"She set up one of her girls to be attacked and she ran away."

Lisa would love nothing more than not put her right, but plays along.

"Wow, that's crazy."

"Yeah, she's vile, proper turning her scabby girls into money machines."

"Yeah, that's horrid. What happened to the girl?"

"Some girl called Lana, or something like that, been in here quite a few times."

Lisa knows she means Layla and was close to blurting it out.

"Anyway, so she was in hospital, then on the run because of some drug lord and now she's pissed off to Australia."

"Australia? When?"

"Yesterday. I only know that because she paid for a bloody taxi to Heathrow Airport. Apparently someone my mate knows was the driver, and she tipped him £30."

"Oh, bet she's happy to go there then. Be a nice holiday in the sun."

"Apparently not, said she ain't coming back, travelling around the whole of OZ, said she will live there."

"Sneaky little cow." Lisa accidentally says.

"Eh?

"Ummm, I meant lucky cow. Would love to go travelling."

Lisa's phone pings, it's Pauline texting, wanting to know if she's found out yet. Once Lisa has replied Pauline comes out early. Morgan asks Lisa if she would like a sun-bed as Pauline is coming out.

"Nah, I was going to have one but I feel a bit unwell, I will come back later." Lisa leaves and does not look at Pauline.

Pauline pauses at reception as Morgan turns her attention to her.

"That was less than 15 minutes."

"Stinks of shit in there, call yourself a manager, clean it up before I ring your area manager."

"Get out, go on, fuck off Pauline, ring them, I don't care."

"That's the spirit. Cheers for reminding me why I never hired you. Unprofessional and bad breath."

"Right leave here, now."

Other customers are arriving as Pauline approaches the door, addressing the customers;
"Be careful of her, she likes to spy on the ladies." Pauline does a licking motion with her tongue. "Ain't that right Morticia."

Morgan picks up her can of coke and throws it at Pauline, but Pauline was too quick to close the glass door and it cracks the glass. Morgan grunts in frustration as Pauline quick steps to catch up with Lisa, feeling proud of herself.

"So, tell me, does she know anything?"

"You're going to flip your lid Polly. I think you better sit down."

"Don't be daft, what did she tell you?"

"She's gone to Australia....to live."

Pauline holds onto a wall and sits down on it.
"You've got to be kidding. You said she's a gossip, maybe she's got it wrong."

"Not this time. She got her name wrong but definitely her. Left yesterday, paid for a taxi to Heathrow, so she's got money."

Pauline gazes into space and thinks things over. Lisa can sense she needs a few minutes to gather herself.

"Right, not a word to anyone."

"Of course not. What an absolute bitch."

"I've got enough in my head to deal with. If Lee gets wind of this. For fuck's sake, she was saying goodbye, I should have cottoned on to that." Pauline holds the side of her head and looks in pain.

"Polly are you alright?" Lisa puts her arm around her.

"These past few weeks have been filled with drama after drama. My nerves are shattered. I don't know if more was put on my plate I would be able to deal with it or choke on it. I'm drained."

"You are the toughest woman I know, you have it in you to

get through this. Just think, this time next week you'll be in a beautiful spot somewhere, in the camper van, with Matthew. That will be calm and peaceful."

"You're right darling, thank you. I will sort my head out later, have a nice long soak in the bath with candles and enjoy the quiet. You go back and help everyone upstairs."

Lisa gives Pauline a hug and Pauline holds her tight for a few seconds.

Back at the Parlour Pauline walks around, room to room, thinking, reminiscing, smiling at memories sparked by each room. Polly's Parlour has been open for 10 years, there's a lot of attachments and emotions to this place. Looking at it all, alone in the quiet, is a first. It's always been vibrant with girls, parties, sex, laughter & tears. Pauline puts the *Massive Attack* album, *Blue Lines* on loudly, bubbles in the bath, a cigarette and a glass of bubbly and relaxes into how she's feeling about life.

Out of the bath an hour later, with towel wrapped around, she answers the Parlour phone.

"Hello Polly's Parlour."

Man on the phone sounds gentle and a bit shy. "Hello, please may I book an appointment? Any time today is fine."

"Yes, I can book you in for 8pm."

"Oh, anything before then? I am only here for the day."

"I am so sorry we are closed for the day, it's a one off, maybe next time when you are here I can get you an early appointment."

Man starts to sound deflated. "I won't ever be coming here again. I can pay extra and I only need body contact, some massage and maybe penetration."

Pauline pauses. She's only done a couple of punters since meeting Matthew because she wants to knock that on the head and will not be doing them after she returns. Life should be enjoying sitting back and running your empire, without the sexual side - that's how she feels. He offers to pay £400 if he could have some time with someone. Pauline has put them all on 'job' and needs those doing, so tells him they are all busy.

"What about you? I've seen lots of Polly's Parlour cards. I would love the chance to visit."

Pauline is looking around, she is moving to a next stage in her life, so feels maybe one last client will be a nice farewell to her working on the game, and a gentle one with massage is the kind of appointment most of them like; its easy and usually sensual. The £400 would be nice in her pocket for the road trip. She thinks about it.

"Hello are you still there?"

"Yes, sorry."

"Yes you will?"

It's amazing money, the temptation, the way it fits to her here and now, pushes her to agree. "Certainly. I will. May I take your name?"

A name in the book is most certainly not a real name usually. She is used to made up names, respecting that most are likely to be cheating or don't want people knowing they pay for sex, but its good to have a name or a nickname to be known by, for the girls, and Pauline.

"Fantastic. I'm Fred."

Pauline rolls her eyes at the basic, generic name, which most seem to give when asked.

"I am only around the corner, see you in a minute."

Him hanging up was a surprise but she looks in the mirror ruffles her damp hair, puts on some lipstick and slips into a white, silk, short dressing gown with fluffy cuffs. Pauline looks fresh, glowing and pretty and greets him with a sultry look, a warm welcoming kiss on the cheek and is pleased he looks nice. In his late 60's, a bit too thin, but comes across as a gentleman. He pays her immediately and apologises for being sweaty.

"I am so sorry, I have walking around the city and sat on the beach in the sun."

"It's a hot day, so all is forgiven. Please, feel free to use the bathroom."
Pauline feels at ease, he has a calming aura of some kind, and eyes that look sad but kind.
"Clean towels in there, do help yourself."

Fred closes the door behind him and she hears the shower go on. Pauline counts the money, it's £40 over, and decides she will be honest with him when he comes out.
Pauline opens her bedroom door wide and lies on her bed and opens her dressing gown, pretending to herself that she's on a photo shoot and working out different poses to greet him with. One is sideways, but doesn't like her profile from the right side. Tries bending over but looks too desperate and seeing her breasts dangling lower than they used to makes her feel like a pregnant dog. Next she tries lying face down and lifting the back of the silk gown half-way past her cheeks, so he would get a glimpse, a teaser, for when he walks in. She feels set, hears the shower go off and the bathroom door open.
The movement on to her front has made Pauline fart loudly, louder than she probably has in her whole life, and is devastated he may have heard. For fear the odour would be too much she grabs her Chanel No.5 and sprays it as many times as possible in the 30 seconds she's got to drown the evidence in perfume before he gets to the door.
Pauline calls him to her room, over compensating on kindness because of her back draft.
"Freddy, in here sweetie."

Old slim Fred walks in and Pauline gasps at how much thinner he looks with no clothes on and because his cock is more horse-like than human.

"Wow Fred, that's some tackle you have there."

Fred seems proud but not in an egoistical way. He throws his clothes onto the floor, trying to be seductive, but his wallet, keys, coins and phone fall out, so kicks it to the side and maintains his stance, with a grin.

He closes the door behind him and walks over to Pauline, caressing her neck with his hands, he pushes her slowly back along the bed and slides onto her. Fred smiles at her and asks her for oil. Pauline grabs some oil she has made a long time ago, lavender and coconut oil, from the bedside drawer and is all set to massage him when he takes the oil and starts rubbing a little of it onto her and asks her quietly to lay back.

The look in his eyes is bright and gives a sense of safeness at his mercy. Fred covers her whole body, between the toes, to ear lobes, caressing each pore as if she was made of fragile diamonds. His big hands and arms at the side of her rib cage, massages her with them, rounding the touch to her buttocks, lifting her a little off the sheets, licking her nipples, pushing her breasts together, the squelching of the oil turning him on even more.

Pauline has gone into a relaxed trance, arching her back and legs shaking as he licks her between the legs and worships every crease, every inch of skin from the top of her thighs to her belly button. This is a euphoric moment she did not expect and feels peaceful knowing this is her last punter ever, a sentimental moment inside for her. Her mind is only filled with a tingling feeling of pure pleasure.

The massage turns into Fred rubbing the end of his cock on her vagina, all around, almost pushing it in, then pulling away, pre-cum drips onto her lips and Fred slides it inside her.

Pauline has not had sex without a condom for a long time. Back in the day when skint, and needing extra money, bareback came at a price and Fred has paid more than enough today. He said it's only once he can come here, he is a lovely man, so all worries are out of the window, so Pauline feels safe.

Pauline has let herself fall into the rare moment of sex, when the pleasure is felt around her whole body, which puts her in a trance like state as she lets Fred not fuck her, but make love to her, passionately.

He makes her sweat, he sweats with her, their lips touch, inside her he is solid, tense and blood in corners of his manhood he never knew existed. Both can feel a connection, the rhythm is in sync, the kissing of her neck makes Pauline wet. This in turn gives Fred muscle throbs, detected by the inside of Pauline, up high, like a new passage has been discovered, breaking all barriers and embracing the rush with legs wide open for both.

In the missionary position Fred's 6ft 3 frame wraps around the back of Pauline, holding her tight, locked and fast breathing and groaning on both parts. No words are needed, the language is spoken through the body, the pain of it feeling so good and not wanting it to end, yet fighting with the sensitivity of Fred inside her, about to explode, almost seems like it's retracting naturally, edging themselves through a lifetime of experience in sex. This unity of such a powerful energy leads to a volcanic level of the release. Still gliding in and out of her, the wetness is splattering and dripping, making them both release more, holding onto the moment they may never feel again. As the grinding becomes slower, the body shakes reduce, and his head comes out from burrowing into her shoulder blade, they both move forwards for one last passionate kiss.

After a cigarette, Fred scoops his clothes up and gets changed, Pauline feels she has gas again, so exits to bathroom and turns the taps on full. She presses a towel against her bum, to cushion the sound, but releases an epic sound - unknown to mankind, on par with how whales communicate. She covers her mouth and cringes.

At reception, as Fred is doing his shoe lace up, Pauline tells him he over paid her.

"You had all I have, as I don't need it anymore."

"Oh, well, thank you. I would say see you again but you said this is the only time you'll be in Brighton?"

"I am, that's right, yes I am..." Fred pauses. "I am actually about to die."

Pauline is so taken back, it catches her breath. "Oh no, Fred. I am so sorry to hear that."

"It's life isn't it. I needed to come and sit on the beach and make my peace with it in my head."

"Did you get what you needed?"

"Yes, I think so. I still have a couple of regrets but, too late now. What you did for me in there, as a man who's dying - just wonderful. I can't thank you enough. Who ever ends up with you will be a lucky man, you're special - always remember that." Pauline wells up, feels for him and gives him the tightest hug. Fred kisses her on the forehead and leaves. Pauline sits on the stool and exhales, deep in thought of what she just experienced. It felt almost spiritual and meant to be.

Pauline sorts the diary, pours some water for herself, then goes to her bedroom to change the sheets. On the floor is Fred's wallet. Pauline runs outside, looks up and down the street but he's not in sight. Back indoors she looks inside to see if there's a phone number or something to track him down. There's no money in there, one bank card and the edge of a pink card. Pauline pulls it out and sees its one of the newer driving licenses. As thought, his name does not say Fred.

Pauline's mind becomes foggy, as if she is looking down on herself, a million thoughts jumble and sends a rush to her blood stream as if it were dry ice engulfing her nervous system. The name is Frank. The pit of Pauline's stomach sets off a panic attack as she sees the Surname, Cochran, and realises her father has just been inside her. The shock is over-whelming, the disbelief puts Pauline into the fetal position, rocking back and forth, crying.

Hours go by, she slips in and out of sleep and tries to work out how she can steer this without telling anyone, ever. He said he had regrets, is at the end of his life, the knowingness she may never see him, or find out if not being in her life was one of his regrets. Having a mixed emotion about a man she thought had no bearing on her life, to now have had him make love to her, and then the over powering sickness of knowing his sperm is inside her. Pauline runs to the bathroom and sits on the toilet, crying quietly.

The Parlour is open, it's 8pm. Pauline will have to face the girls at some point soon, but looks horrendous and it's obvious she has been through something emotional. To be completely satisfied by her own father, to know she loved it, stirs up a deep twisted battle with herself to hold it together and process it.

The girls are sounding happy and a knock on the bathroom door from Maddie, screaming her head off about something, gives Pauline a break from her thoughts and calls out; "Two minutes."

Pauline knows in her heart that he did not know who she was, she knows men, she knows when men are in deep and into the stranger danger arena of feelings, there's a certain look, how he reacted in the way men act and position themselves when it's a new experience with an unknown. She's been at this for far too many years not to be able to know that.

Shaking and reaching for a Valium out of the cabinet, she quickly applies a face pack on, to disguise the evidence, and swings open the door to greet Maddie, as if she was opening a concert show; "Here I am!"

Maddie isn't in the mood to care, she is fuming.
"Who broke my bloody hoist?"

Pauline shrugs her shoulders and feels guilty. Lisa appears and has the balls to speak up.

Lisa tries to console her but Maddie is hyperventilating and staring at the floor. Lisa looks at Pauline and does not know how to deal with Maddie, Pauline offers no help because she is clinging on for dear life inside for her mental state to remain stable and have strength over her barrier she has up for this evening.

When Maddie comes up for air, Lisa hands her a tissue and rubs her back.

"I was hoping to surprise you with a swanky new one today but the delivery man let me down."

Pauline looks at Lisa in shock, knowing she is making this

up. Lisa mouths the words - "What can I say?" with shrugged shoulders.

Maddie is calming a little, but instead of waiting for more news of Lisa's imaginary hoist, Maddie needs to share how hard she worked for that hoist. The NHS were dragging their heels to get her one so she sold her mum's clothes and did lots of "Platinum Punters." Immediately Lisa's ears prick up

"What are they?"

Maddie gains some composure. "Men with more bank cards than brain cells, parting with mega money for lots of urinary delights. The amount of times I've gone nearly gone as rusty as Tin Man from Wizard of OZ in this chair, from being piddled on so many times."

Lisa was about to laugh, she looks at Pauline and can feel something is off kilter.

"Polly, are you OK?"

"Yes I am dandy darlings, just a little tired. Going to have an early night."

"So, what happened to my hoist?"

Lisa's quick thinking she delivers with complete confidence.

Pauline takes a step back and looks on at Lisa, at how far she has come and what she has been through.

Lisa continues. "I had a client who saw you on the website and when he read about the hoist it turned him on. He asked to have a go and I let him lay back in it and it collapsed. He has given me £50 towards it but I wanted to get you the newer model."

"Lisa they are about a grand, I need that, it's my business tool. You lot can sit on top, jump around, do 69'ers, do what you want. I am limited, but the hoist gives me freedom to at least do other positions than the fucking vegetable pose."

Lisa feels terrible and promises to do more work and get her one by the end of the week. "I'll have to go back to Beryls barn and let Colin turn me into a Lama if need be. I promise you I will get it."

Maddie is finding it hard to smile or cheer up. "It's come at the wrong time, this is a depressing time for me."

Pauline extends her sympathy. "Maddie, I am so sorry to hear that. What's the matter?"

"You and my dad off for a month, means..."
Maddie starts crying again.

"It means I have to put up with carers from an agency driving me, showering me, bringing me here. I am so embarrassed. Dad does most for me, probably through guilt, but I only like one carer from the agency but she's part-time. I can't bear strangers helping me wash. It's degrading."

Sandra is in the doorway listening in, and feeling sorry for Maddie, even though they clash. Sandra has a total light bulb moment.

"I've got an idea - could she stay here whilst you're away Polly? That means you would be here and not need to be carried in for work."

Usually this would be a point-blank no, but with what she is fighting with internally and knowing Maddie's dad will be away with her, she doesn't have the heart to quash that idea.
"Yes, of course. How will that solve the problem though?"

Immediately Maddie has jumped to the conclusion Sandra is being fake and may offer that the girls all wash her in the mornings.
"Forget it Sange, stay away from my fange."

"I wouldn't go down there, even with rubber gloves on. I can imagine how cave-like it is down there." Sandra laughing, thinking they would all find that funny, but it's all still.

Maddie's eye balls look they are about to burst, says nothing.

"Look, I know of at least two different men in my own my black book who would pay to do that in the mornings on their way to work. They will pay you, so win-win, right?"

Maddie feels at war with her mind. Accepting an offer like that from Sandra would be like a bitter pill to swallow, but knows this is golden.

"To be fair, that's actually genius Sandra. Polly, is that ok with you?"

"Of course, it would be lovely for Matthew to know everything is sorted. Sandra, if I can leave that with you to arrange, thank you."

Maddie cheers up and shakes Sandra's hand. "Cheers, I really appreciate that. I would have been so depressed for a month."

"Anything for the less fortunate, and if they let me down I'm a dab hand with a flannel and a bar of soap." Sandra loving her own sense of humour. Everyone is smiling, apart from Maddie.

"See what I mean. Why do you have to be such a bitch with back handed comments."

"It's alright for you to make jokes but when I do it you get shitty. Fine, you know what, I won't ring my gentleman, stay at home with the qualified disability carers." Sandra walks off and Maddie sulks.

Pauline needs to take her first tough stance against Maddie, she can't be seen to favour her and it feels like Maddie is acting like she's got rights, being Matthews daughter. She has held her own feelings together long enough today also, time to snap.

"Young lady, you need to know which side your bread is buttered. I will not have you feeling sorry for yourself here. She's right, you do take the piss out of yourself, and others. Learn to take it or work somewhere else. Be grateful and go and accept her offer - and apologise."

Maddie is shocked but quiet. She never thought Pauline would crack like that, so wheels herself off and grovels to Sandra, whos on the loo.

"Sandra, I am sorry. Honestly it's a lovely gesture and I would like to accept."

"Come on in why don't you. I'll sort it. I want 15%."

"Fair enough. Cheers."

Maddie agrees only because without this she is trapped, but feels repelled to ask; "What exactly is your problem with me? One minute you're kind, then you're nasty."

"Barging in whilst I am taking a piss is one extra reason now. You remind me of someone I don't like, not always, just certain traits."

"Who is that?"

"My late gran. I lived with her until she died, she was in a chair too. Treated me like a slave, did fuck all for herself and left me nothing in her will. Sometimes you remind me of her, your attitude."

"Well I'm not your gran."

"You smell like her though."

"Violets?"

"No, piss."

"See what I mean, you're so..."

"Take a bloody joke Maddie. This whole princess thing is getting draining. You are NOT a real princess, so get off your...I was gonna say high horse, but that's insensitive, there's no way you could get on a horse."

"Actually I rode side-saddle in a disability sports day once."

"You need leg and thigh grip to ride, how did you stay up?"

"They tied my legs together and around the saddle." Sandra and Maddie giggle together and breaks the tension.

"You've got balls Maddie, you make me laugh. I do like you, you're like an annoying little sister."

"You're like an overbearing grandmother."

"Touché lil' bitch princess. I'm sorry Maddie. I had a hard life being brought up by an obnoxious grandmother in a wheelchair. Lots of things about you in that chair sets me off."

"It's ok, I understand. Would it help if I sprayed it a different colour?"

"What colour?"

"Pink. We could call it the PPPP = Pimp up Princess' Pink Project."

Sandra laughs along with Maddie. Sandra takes her hand. "I am a moody cow some days, just ignore me."

"That'll be easy!" Maddie manoeuvers herself out of the bathroom, goes to her room and stays overnight.

Matthew brings loads of Maddie's belongings over for her and stays a few hours with Pauline. Pauline tries the breathing techniques she learned in therapy whilst dealing with the trauma of her father. A life of being battered gives Pauline an armour and resilience she is able to get from her emotional reserve tank and use it to connect with Matthew, park it and deal with it later.

Pauline and Matthew are like children; giggling, cracking jokes, chasing her down the hallway and tickling her. They go shopping to stock on goods for the road trip, make sure all plans and details are sorted and the camper is full of fuel and some cash. Pauline looks at all she has, the Parlour, Matthew, the girls, no debts, friends and good health. Bringing that fully into her awareness, reminding herself of these parts, gives her the ability to enjoy the here and now, no one would ever know what she has been through lately. Appreciating some light which is within the darkness, keeps any dents to her sanity at arms length. Pauline is grabbing life by the balls, no matter at what cost.

The following day is Gary's funeral. Pauline is dressed in a black Chanel pencil skirt with short cropped black jacket, gold embroidery around the edge, a black hat with veil, black fishnet tights, black 5" black stilettos with a gold heel. Herself and Lisa are about to leave, Lee rings Polly's mobile. Pauline looks like the colour is draining from her face, Lisa overhears her,

"Call me again in five minutes when I am out of here." Pauline looks at Lisa, "I'll fill you in on the way."

Pauline addresses the girls who are on shift today. "Got to dash, see you in a couple of hours OK girls."

Natalie, Sheila, Sandra and Leigh get up and kiss Pauline on the cheek. Maddie offers, "I would get up but, you know." Points to her legs.

"Come here you." Pauline pulls her chair forward and kisses Maddie on the forehead.

"The 2 become 1 song was made for you and my dad. He is lucky to have you."

"I know he is." Pauline smiles and re-applies a bit more lipstick. "Right, off we go Lisa."

Pauline and Lisa leave the Parlour and head off in Pauline's car. As Pauline is driving to the cemetery, she pulls over to take another call from Lee.

"Hey, fill me in."

Pauline is nodding, biting the side of her mouth, seems shocked. After this quick call Pauline turns to Lisa.

"Dean and Harry couldn't have killed Gary, they were out of the country, they've got evidence."

"Oh my God, seriously?

"My head is spinning. I don't know what to think."

Pauline looks at a nearby building whilst she's pausing in thought, sees Jake walking out, followed by Belinda. Lisa is saying something to her but Pauline has zoned out, laser focused on seeing where they go. Pauline starts the car and spins off to follow them round the corner. Lisa still chatting.

"Lisa sshh a minute. Look." Pauline points to Jake and Belinda walking off.

"I didn't know they were mates."

"Saw them last week sat outside Suzie's cafe. Told me he only just met her. Lying little skank."

"Let's follow, we've got plenty of time."

Pauline slowly turns the corner to side street, Lisa still talking.

POLLY'S PARLOUR

"You don't have blood on your hands, whatever has happened. And from what you've told me he was vermin anyway Polly."

"That's not the point, it would mean it may have been someone else. Someone is gonna come looking for Robert one day, that'll be a mess."

Pauline has pulled over behind a van because Jake and Belinda have got into a Black Audi. Aware of the time, Pauline is reluctant to follow but the urge is too strong.

For 10 minutes Pauline is two cars behind and sees them turn into a one way street, and park up but don't get out.

Pauline parks a few car spaces behind. The cars are in between but being in a Range Rover, means she can see more, as she's higher up, and can see them laughing, so she phones his mobile. Pauline sees him pick the phone up and look, then put it back in his pocket, so she calls again, and again. On the fourth call Jake picks it up and puts on a sleepy voice as if he's just woken up whilst yawning loudly.

"Mmm Morning. Jesus, what time is it?"

"Hey darling, aww sorry have I woken you up?"

"Yeah had a late night. Was up with Julia and Emma and Adams apple until 4am."

Pauline decides to wind him up and improvises a scenario on the spot.

"So, you remember last week you met that Belinda, the one you called a drag queen?"

Pauline can see him looking shifty in the car and loves she has the upper hand.

"You need to be really careful, everyone is talking about it. She's got some virus, lots of people who have slept with her, including clients, have come to me after being unwell. Two were rigged up to oxygen tanks."

"What? Hang one a sec, let me open my bedroom window and let some fresh air in here."

242

Jake opens car door very quietly and steps outside. It's a quiet street so the sound marries with the bullshit he's sprouting with Pauline.

"Are you sure this ain't a rumour?"

"It's fact, seriously. You know she does all the kinky work, the dirty stuff. I bet she's riddled."

Jake looks in through car window, does a strained grin at Belinda and shrugs his shoulders.

"I don't know what to say."

"Just wanted to make sure I am looking out for you, like I do my girls. Momma Polly will always be here for you."

Jake looks like he feels sick with guilt. "Same Polly. Thanks for the heads up. I think I am going to go back to sleep for a bit."

"Hang on." Pauline looks at Lisa and smirks. "I am on my way up the stairs, got some cards to drop off for you."

Jake goes red, looks beside himself and paces, doesn't know what to say. "Umm, oh, I am not in my flat. No, no, I stayed out last night."

"You just said you were up until 4am with the girls."

"Yeah, yeah, I went to stay with someone after."

"Oh, I see. Bless you Jake. I will let you get back to sleep and I will speak to you later."

"Okie Dokie Polly."

"Bye darling."

As soon as Jake gets into car, Belinda starts it, driving off at a steady speed.

Lisa wondering. "How did you just keep your cool?"

"I am raging Lisa." Pauline waits until she sees the car leave the end of the street, and pulls out herself and drives off. Pauline sends a text to him, which reads; "Love your red vest by the way. Looks lovely with those denim shorts.

She knows this will freak him out.

In Belinda's car Jake bends the truth a bit.

"Polly was asking me about shifts, then got weird. She knows I was lying. She's seen me, not sure where or how, but she's just text she likes my clothes, so has seen me. This was clean on this morning. I'm freaking out now."

"If only she knew we would always have her back. She's too suspicious of people for her own good."

"I actually feel terrible now. If she's seen me with you, she will go wild."

Belinda puts her hand on top of his and squeezes it tight. "We've got each other. Everything will work out, I know so."

Jake looks at Belinda, with a worried expression.

"I hope so babe."

Pauline is driving faster than the limit, back streets, not stopping for anyone, everyone has to pull over for her and even drives through a red light. Because she can't stand being late, for anything.

"I need to find out why he's with Belinda, Lisa."

Lisa thinks it's brilliant. "I can do some digging. Gossip Morgan probably knows, if anyone knows it'll be her. I love this, it feels like we are undercover detectives. Let's follow more." Lisa texts Morgan.

"We can't, maybe later. Shouldn't have trusted him." Hurry up with that text, I need to know."

"You have been true to yourself, that's all that matters. You look out for people, especially us girls. We owe our lives to you, seriously Polly. Jake can get lost. This could be the start of a new chapter with you going off travelling tomorrow with Matthew. Get today out the way and enjoy the fresh air after all you've been through. I won't let you down. I want you to feel relaxed whilst you're away, so you enjoy every minute of it."

"Trust me, he will not be working for me by the end of today, so you won't need to worry about him. I know you won't let me down, thanks darling, and thank you for coming with me today. I have always wanted to do a trip like this, that's one thing off my bucket list. I can't wait to have some peace, my head needs it."

Pauline arrives at the cemetery and pulls into a parking space. "Look at these lot, half of them look like they have come up from the graves themselves. Let's sit here for a minute, go over when the hearse pulls in, not in the mood for small talk."

"Bet you'll be glad when this day is over, I know I will be."

Lisa's phone bleeps, it's a text from Morgan.

"Ugh gross, they are shagging." Lisa looks shocked. "Polly, apparently they are at it together, so Morgan reckons."

"That's repulsive, another liar. I hope she really is riddled now. I cannot have bell-ends boyfriend working for me, no chance. Lisa you are really going to have to hold the fort with strength, be my eyes and ears."

"I will, you know I never let you down. Andy and his mate for support will be great for me, will make me feel safe."

"Andy will be a rock, he has my back, always. He knows he needs to be here for you. Let's get this over with, go to the wake for an hour and chat with Lee, then pack my clothes and essentials for an early morning off into the sunset and right up to the north coast 500. Probably stop half-way, park by a lake, or a forest. It's going to bring me and Matthew closer, I can feel it."

"You look perfect together. I love this for you, it's about time. Oh the hearse is coming."

Lisa and Pauline quickly get out of car, link arms and head over to the grave side.

When the burial is taking place, with about 50 people stood around, the coffin gets lowered into the ground and Pauline feels emotional, so takes Lisa's hand. Through her veil, Pauline locks eyes with Lee and he gives her a slight smile, Pauline half smiles and looks down.

As the vicar is reading words from his bible, and the sun shines, Pauline's focus is taken away by a black car, with blacked out windows, driving past very slowly.

Pauline lifts her veil to wipe a tear and as the back window comes down, Pauline squints because of the sun reflecting on the car and not positive she is seeing clearly. Pauline looks at the coffin, looks back at the car, with a dozen thoughts cramming her head, and a small smile at the side of her mouth, the one which is barely visible, but means the world.

There's a female in the back, on her own, snorting a line of coke off of her clenched fist, giving a nod and a wink to Pauline - it's Nicki.

Pauline pulls the black veil back down over her face and bows her head.

The End.

For further info or enquiries; spiritualee2024@yahoo.com

ACKNOWLEDGEMENT

Cheers to the decent folk who gave their eyes to this before going to print. Not all Karen's are chaotic. Thank you xx

Thank you to Emma Jade Reed photography, Dorset, UK.

ABOUT THE AUTHOR

Lee West

After a few years of acting, Lee studied script analysis in New York. Polly's Parlour was Lee's first script to come after the training, but the depth of this story could not be diluted down into a shortened version.

Polly needed pages and this first instalment will let you peek into a life where real souls graft and will lead your imagination to place where laughter can exist in the roughest of days.

Written in a way which is not crass, considering its adult content, but where you immerse yourself into a world where you form your own personal connection with the people who work in the adult industry, by seeing what life is also like outside of work. The drama is fast paced, the events are mind blowing & the story is riddled with feelings and emotions. Lee's style of writing is honest, to the point and has dark humour embedded throughout.

AFTERWORD

Polly's Parlour 2 is already in progress.

Printed in Great Britain
by Amazon

45830832R00145